"Let the children have their night of fun and laughter.
Let the gifts of Father Christmas delight their play.
Let us grown-ups share to the full in their unstinted
pleasures before we turn again to the stern task and the
formidable years that lie before us, resolved that, by our
sacrifice and daring, these same children shall not be
robbed of their inheritance or denied their right
to live in a free and decent world. And so, in
God's mercy, a happy Christmas to you all."

—WINSTON CHURCHILL

WHISTLE STOP Café MYSTERIES

WINTER WEATHER

JENELLE HOVDE

Whistle Stop Café Mysteries is a trademark of Guideposts.

Published by Guideposts
100 Reserve Road, Suite E200
Danbury, CT 06810
Guideposts.org

Cover and interior design by Müllerhaus
Cover illustration by Greg Copeland, represented by Illustration Online LLC.
Typeset by Aptara, Inc.

ISBN 978-1-961251-78-6 (hardcover)
ISBN 978-1-961251-79-3 (epub

Printed and bound in the United States of America
10 9 8 7 6 5 4 3 2 1

WINTER WEATHER

Jason Hovde, *tí amo*.

ITALIAN VOCABULARY

bistrot • a small café

buona madre • good mother

chiacchiere • fried pastries shaped like angel wings

Il Duce • "The Leader," a nickname for Mussolini

Il Secondo Futurismo • the second future, a new world order envisioned by Mussolini and pictured via the arts

mia cara • my dear

mia carissima • my dearest

nonna • grandmother

Opera Nazionale Balilla • youth program for the National Fascist Party, containing the **balilla** for boys ages eight to fourteen, then the **avanguardisti** for boys ages fourteen to eighteen

orti di guerra • war gardens

per favore • please

polizia • the police

resistenza • the resistance against the Fascist party

ti amo • I love you

CHAPTER ONE

Nico Carosi took a shuddering breath as he studied the stolen paintings spread haphazardly over the table inside the police station. The frames were splintered and chipped, suggesting that the art had been pried off the walls, as if it had resisted the act of violence to the bitter end. Art ripped from Jewish families or Italian aristocracy who openly defied Mussolini.

Nico swallowed hard, his mouth dry, as he glanced at the nearest piece, a sketch. His hand hovered over the aged paper curling at the edges, yet he dared not touch the masterful lines of a weeping father clasping his adult son. The Return of the Prodigal Son *by Rembrandt.*

Someone had been careless this time. The paper bore evidence of a fresh tear. There was a splash on the left corner, staining the paper brown, like a stray tear-drop. There was a wrinkle too, as if someone had clung to it to prevent its inevitable removal.

He flinched. Who had owned this piece, and where were they now?

"Well?" a sharp, nasal voice demanded. "How much is it worth?"

He whirled around to find the captain watching him. The man's oiled black mustache twitched.

Nico exhaled slowly. He was indeed an artist, hired to paint monstrosities for his country—or rather, propaganda posters. He was also called in to assess any pieces taken "for the good of the Italian empire." This was to be a new Roman Empire intended to rival any former Caesar's rule.

"It's worth a great deal. How much, I don't know yet. But one of your—" He bit his tongue to keep from saying his thoughts out loud. One of your goons. He cleared his throat. "One of your men ripped the sketch, and I cannot fix it."

The captain gave an exasperated sigh as he prowled closer. With the precise click of his polished boots, he halted beside Nico, close enough to press against his shoulder as if they were friends. As if his mere presence didn't send chills up and down Nico's spine.

Nico suppressed a shudder at the captain's proximity. The black uniform with silver trim made Nico feel lightheaded with fear.

"I assumed it was a Rembrandt sketch," the captain said with a pompous sniff as he eyed the aged paper with his hands clasped behind his back. "The old woman swore it wasn't and tried to take it back. Do not blame my men for the damage. I have my orders to retrieve anything of value. Everything belongs to Mussolini, especially now that he has returned to power and will deal with any remaining traitors. As you well know, the state demands the immediate return of any historic Italian treasure."

A woman then. Rich once and still deserving of dignity. Perhaps someone like Nico's white-haired nonna, who used to slip him a small basket of cannoli when sugar and cream had been plentiful.

Nico's hands curled into tight fists at his sides. He forced his fingers to relax and slipped his hand into his pocket to finger the blunt pencil stub tucked inside. His mind swirled with questions about the fate of the sketch's owner, but it would do no good to ask. Mussolini, after a failed coup, had exacted a terrible revenge on the country, including his own son-in-law. The authorities would not tolerate impertinent questions this season, and Captain Accardo was Mussolini's man through and through.

Nico moved to the next table, examining a small marble bust of a woman. Her cheeks were smooth and round. Like Sophia's.

But he would not think of Sophia at this moment. Could not, when six guards and their captain watched his every move. Any hint of a vulnerability such as fondness could prove fatal for him as well as the object of his affections.

"This is more modern, I think, but in the style used in ancient Greece." He removed his hand from his pocket and lifted the sculpture, noting the signature beneath the bust. "It's by Adolfo Wildt, an Italian artist. You can commission his work even now. I studied with him three years ago."

"I assumed it was much older." The captain bristled, his cheeks flushing as Nico placed the bust back on the table. "I suppose I will need to dispose of it if it has no value."

"On the contrary, the bust is worth something," Nico replied softly. He kept his tone even. Any eagerness would betray his anxiety to save precious artworks like the sculpture, and they would destroy it for that alone. "Wildt is well respected."

Ten years before, several artists had banded together, envisioning another renaissance of expression. Il Secondo Futurismo, *Second Futurism. Unlike Hitler,*

Mussolini had claimed to envision a world of art that allowed different styles to flourish, particularly those that echoed ancient Greece and Rome. But the promised freedom of expression had been a lie, like all of Mussolini's other lies about peace and prosperity and justice.

Nico moved toward another table but stopped when the captain snatched his arm, hard fingers digging into the tender flesh.

"You do not wish me to assess these?" Nico gestured to the vibrant painting resting against the table.

"Those are to be burned. Filthy pieces painted by the resistenza."

The cubist painting, stacked with several others, practically glowed with geometric red and orange, with each stroke slashed across the canvas as if rage had propelled the paintbrush. Yet the image was simple to discern as Rome on fire. The symbolic image repulsed Nico too, but perhaps not for the same reasons as the captain. He knew of his fellow artists, who had painted caricatures of Mussolini during the leader's arrest and paid the price. Such defiance. Such boldness. Did these artists now languish in a jail or a camp reserved for dissidents? Or worse?

He averted his gaze from the riot of angry colors, pulling his arm free of the captain's grip. "Then it appears my work here is done."

"You will, of course, bring your latest posters to me for review." The captain brushed a finger against his mustache as if he managed the finest of museums.

"In two weeks' time," Nico replied. He hated the posters commissioned to recruit more men for the war effort, especially now that German troops had rescued Mussolini from his recent captivity.

The resistance had attempted a coup back in September and failed. Allies pushed into Sicily and advanced farther into Italy while Rome crawled with SS guards. Now, Nico painted to remind the Roman populace of the "illustrious future," should they stay the course. The latest prints comprised monstrosities of angular lines meant to mimic the fierce Roman gods. What good did such art do when children went hungry and men felt the weight of a ruthless government?

"You will do it sooner." The captain's command fell over the hushed room while the uniformed men continued to watch Nico with suspicion.

He nodded once before exiting the storage room of the police station, a place originally meant for justice, not robbery. But Mussolini's secret police, the OVRA—or Organization for Vigilance and Repression of Anti-Fascism—saw no irony in their actions. They kept files on over a hundred thousand residents, focusing on

Rome, but with tightening control sweeping across the country at Hitler's insistence.

Nico straightened his coat, preparing for the bitter wind outside the station, which brought a few rare flakes of snow. He might even have enjoyed the first sign of winter weather if not for the low voices he heard in the storage room.

"The chief of police has ordered another sweep of the area tonight," the captain murmured to the other men.

Nico paused in the dingy hallway, not daring to breathe so he could hear the rest of the conversation. Yet what could he do? A shiver rippled through him at the mention of the chief of the secret police. Nico knew Matteo Verga better than he might have wished, as they'd gone to school together.

"Arrest anyone caught with the resistenza and anyone Jewish, or we will answer to the chief of police," the captain ordered from the storage room.

Fidgeting with his scarf, Nico paused longer than he ought, hoping to hear who might be the next target. No one deserved to fall into the hands of his old school-mate. But as Nico fiddled with his coat on the pretense of buttoning it up, one policeman headed for the open door, grinding to a halt when his dark gaze collided with Nico's. The policeman narrowed his eyes in a silent threat.

Nico fled the station, escaping into the approaching night. The sky above lay like an iron curtain, dark and foul. He tugged up the collar of his coat as he rushed down the familiar streets until at last he found one cobblestone lane lined with shops closing for the night.

Dare he pray for the safety of the next victims? Or would God refuse to listen, as He usually seemed to these days? Did miracles exist anywhere during this Christmas season?

Nico found no answer as the wind continued to whip through the street and the meager sunlight faded into twilight. He hurried toward his home, a small flat where the living room served as his studio, right above a struggling leather goods store.

The scent of fresh bread lingered in the air, a siren call that made his stomach rumble loudly. Plunging a hand through his hair, Nico stopped in front of a glass window covered with the smudged fingerprints of hungry children.

The Giudice Bakery. He peered into the shadowy depths, looking for her. But only his gaunt reflection, replete with wild curls, stared back at him.

Yet he strained for a single glimpse of Sophia Giudice, who in better days had helped her father,

Angelo, stock the loaves and set out trays of sugar-coated chiacchiere—*fried pastries shaped like angel wings*—*crispy cannoli oozing with vanilla cream, or buttery Italian wedding cookies that melted in his mouth. Such treats were now reserved for Hitler's best men.*

When Nico earned extra money from the posters, he worked up the courage to purchase her biscotti. However, during his last visit, an officer had complimented Nico's mural in the nearest gymnasium. Sophia had cast him a baleful glare that had turned the hard cookie studded with pistachios to ash on his tongue.

The shop appeared silent and shadowed this evening. They must have closed while Nico had examined the stolen paintings on behalf of the regime. Giudice served everyone, but the average Italian could hardly afford anything but rice these days. The officers, on the other hand, often came to the bakery to buy the white bread, even as they sneered in disdain at the baker. Nico was sure Sophia hated them.

Perhaps she hated him too, and how could he blame her?

His throat tightened as he pushed away from the glass and trudged up the narrow stairs of the next building to his flat. He unlocked the door, eased out of his threadbare jacket, and slung it across the nearest chair.

The apartment appeared extra dreary this evening. He fumbled for a match and struck it, listening to the hiss as it flared to life. After lighting the gas lamp, he sank down onto the kitchen chair, more miserable than he could ever remember being. All around the cramped room, posters in bright red and black hung on the walls, screaming for his attention. He couldn't escape the Fascist party if he tried. Hadn't his older brother warned him to leave Italy back in the '30s, before it was too late?

Now Alberto lived in America, no doubt running a restaurant with a pretty wife and plenty of children. Why had he and Alberto fought over where home was? Why hadn't his brother stayed in Rome to help him look after their aging nonna? Surely anyone would understand that Nico could never leave the city if their grandmother refused to abandon her beloved home. Yet now she was gone too, leaving him alone in the flat. Alone and trapped.

What a shame to let the months slip into years, with nothing but silence stretching between him and his remaining family. Nico dragged a palm across his face. Despite the memory of his nonna's voice reminding him to find something to be thankful for, the joy of Christmas was nowhere to be found in his heart. Years later, he still missed Alberto's ready smile and equally ready advice.

Was he destined to be alone forever? Nico's eyes watered as endless regrets threatened to drown him.

A small painting waited on the easel, the soft colors soothing against the red and black posters. His sole act of rebellion. The Madonna cradled the Christ child and gazed back at him with luminous brown eyes, while the faint light of the star lined her hair and face with silver. A painting of hope and joy. Of tenderness.

He could almost imagine her whisper, "You carry such a heavy burden, Nico. Lay it down."

And so he did his best to obey, choosing to lose himself in rich indigo and celestial silver. He picked up the nearest brush, the bristles stiff despite the recent cleaning, and reached for his oil paints.

His hand froze as a frantic knock sounded on the front door.

CHAPTER TWO

*S*now fell softly outside the Whistle Stop Café, just as the forecast had predicted for this brisk Friday morning. Debbie Albright parked her car beside the old train station, now converted into a café and museum.

For a blissful moment, she sat within the warm cocoon of the driver's seat, taking in the charming scene of a station that had seen thousands of soldiers pass through during World War II. If she closed her eyes, she could almost hear the faint sound of the big band music playing over the loudspeaker. She could see the soldiers hurrying across the platform with doughnuts in hand while tearful family and friends waved goodbye, wondering when they would see each other again.

She switched off the ignition. She was feeling especially nostalgic and excited. Perhaps it was because of the recent plans she and Greg Connor had made for Christmas. In the past, she had spent Christmas alone with her family, especially after her fiancé, Reed Brandt, had been killed in action over twenty years before. Now in her early forties, she had thought a new relationship unlikely—until this year.

She slowly exhaled. She felt both excited and nervous. Greg had two teenage sons, Jaxon and Julian. She had never dated a man with kids before. The boys—Jaxon especially—had taken a while to warm up to the idea of their dad dating after their mother's passing several years before. Would she be able to give them a good Christmas, or would she still feel like an intruder?

She batted the troublesome thought aside. She had so much to be thankful for. Why let worry creep in during the holidays? Instead, she would focus on the source of her happiness.

Perhaps her current joy was because she had finally found her place of belonging as a restaurant owner in the small town of Dennison, Ohio, a far cry from the lonely city and her former corporate job. And the Whistle Stop Café would be featured on the popular TV show *Days of Yesteryear* as a Christmas special, thanks to the interest of a famous historian and rising social media star, Maurice Devons, who had landed the ultimate TV deal. He filmed historical sites across the United States and featured antiques with unique history. He planned to focus on the history of soldiers traveling through the station.

The air outside the car was crisp, and as she unlocked the door to the café, she heard her business partner, Janet, singing in the kitchen. Debbie took care of the details of running the café while Janet's baking lured visitors from near and far.

Janet's rendition of "Deck the Halls" rang through the cheerful café, where each table featured a lantern filled with twinkling lights. The spicy scents of cinnamon and ginger with a hint of orange wafted through the air. The previous week, Debbie and Janet had replaced the gingham tablecloths with a charming plaid print and added real greenery entwined with ribbon across the windows and along the countertops. Well, half of the planned greenery was up anyway. The Christmas decorations had been more expensive than Debbie expected, but they were worth it considering that the Whistle Stop Café was about to go national.

Last night, she and Janet had giggled over the phone like giddy schoolgirls as they went over their plans for the ultimate Christmas celebration to present Dennison in the limelight. The train station would run a special ride, offering a Nativity play for the guests, while live Nativity animals would attract interest outside in the parking lot. Kim Smith, director of the museum, was overseeing it all.

Local artists would display their best Christmas art in the café. Ricky Carosi, the owner of Buona Vita, had promised to add his family's most treasured possession to the collection—a Nativity painting. Debbie's mother, Becca, had wondered if they might go viral thanks to Janet's simple but luxurious baking and the charming ambience of the Whistle Stop Café.

Debbie found her friend pulling a tray of gingerbread men and women from the oven, the cookies a perfect golden brown.

"Today is the day, Janet."

Janet glanced over her shoulder as she set the tray down to cool, her cheeks flushed. "Yes, it is. But I'm behind schedule. Ian's got a sore throat and a nasty cough. I made him stay home. Believe me, he's got plenty of that stubborn Scottish attitude. He actually tried to argue with me, telling me, 'Dinna werry yer head aboot it. A policeman always knows his dooty.'" Janet's exasperation softened. "There's something about colds and flus that brings out the accent."

"It's adorable, but you don't need a sick family over the holidays. Poor guy. Ian always puts in so many hours. He needs a good, long break."

Janet nodded emphatically. "Exactly. We need everyone healthy."

"If you made some of your chicken noodle soup, he'll be back on his feet in no time. I'm convinced your soup has magic powers."

"I'll send some of it home with you," Janet said. "Would you mind terribly if I left early this afternoon to go check on him? And can you finish the greenery in the café this morning? You'll find the box on one of the tables."

"I can close the café, and I can decorate. No problem at all." Debbie saluted before removing her heavy coat to hang on a nearby hook. She slipped on her Christmas apron, a red-and-white affair that reminded her of a candy cane. As she tied the strings around her waist, she heard a ding in her purse beside her coat. She pulled out her cell phone and found a text from Greg.

Call me when you're free? It's about Christmas.

She grinned as she texted him back. Sure thing, but first I have to finish decorating the café before the TV crew gets here.

You're going to be the next big thing. I can feel it. Maybe I'll swing by for coffee so you don't have to add something else to your to-do list. Plus, I'll take any excuse to see you.

Debbie grinned as she slipped her phone into her pants pocket. She loved that Greg was so open with his affection, to say nothing of his thoughtfulness.

Humming under her breath, she lifted the fragrant greens out of the cardboard box as a silver Lexus sedan pulled up to the café, gleaming in the winter sunlight. A man eased out of the car, pausing to study the station. He appeared to be in his late twenties or early thirties, with shaggy blond hair. He wore a rust-colored corduroy blazer with patches at the elbows and a gray scarf looped around his neck. He needed a few vintage books pinned beneath his arm to complete the professor style.

Two other men climbed out the other side of the vehicle. One was a nondescript middle-aged man in a beige parka. The other, who seemed to be in his fifties, wore a black cowboy hat rimmed with silver and a pheasant feather. His black leather fringed jacket, black sweater, and matching denim jeans provided a stark contrast against the fresh snow. As he walked around the car, pointing at the building, she spotted crimson snakeskin cowboy boots on his feet—boots that told her exactly who he was.

Maurice Devons—the eccentric collector who made a career of finding obscure and often overlooked historical pieces worth a small fortune—was standing in front of her café.

Debbie checked the clock. Wasn't he supposed to come later in the morning, after eleven? He must have a reason for arriving hours early.

She had gobbled up his latest season, especially the series providing tips for those who wanted to style their antiques in more modern ways. His folksy charm and rugged good looks were enough to give any interior design show a run for its money. His brand of chalk paint for giving vintage pieces new life was available in nearly every major store.

As Debbie watched the three men, Maurice blew on his hands, his breath a steady stream of fog in the morning light. He beamed as he pointed to the building. The younger man in the rust-colored jacket followed Maurice's gaze as he pulled a large satchel from the car. The man in the beige coat tugged his hood closer.

Gulping, she glanced at the greenery in her hands before setting the garland on the nearest seat. Decorating would have to wait for now. She hadn't expected Maurice to come so early in the day, but he'd certainly chosen the perfect moment with the early sunrise coating the surrounding snowbanks in rose hues. Plump flakes floated in the air, bringing an ethereal touch as the rising sun caught them and transformed them into silver glitter.

"Janet, he's here. Maurice Devons is outside our café." Debbie hurried back to the kitchen, where her friend mixed the royal icing for the gingerbread men.

Janet's eyes widened. "But he's early."

"Yes. He's most certainly at our doorstep, and he's even wearing his crimson boots."

For once, Janet, who ran the kitchen with cool efficiency, seemed absolutely frazzled. "I was going to put on makeup and do something with my hair before he came."

"You are always beautiful. You have nothing to worry about."

Janet chuckled weakly as she rubbed her nose, leaving a trail of flour. "Normally, I would bask in the glow of your compliments, but our faces are going to be plastered everywhere, and I've got these awful bags under my eyes because I couldn't sleep last night. Besides, these cookies won't decorate themselves."

Debbie snatched a paper towel and approached her friend. "Here, let me get that flour on your nose. Unless you think we should leave it for authenticity."

Janet groaned.

Debbie swiped away the white smudge. "There we go. We probably have some time before he talks to us. He'll probably scout the area for the perfect camera angles first."

Her words calmed her own mind, and Janet seemed to relax a little as well. Debbie resumed her tasks in the front of the café with brisk efficiency. She finished arranging the last of the boughs near the glass countertop as Maurice entered the café. Then, any tranquility she had managed to cultivate fled.

Maurice tipped his cowboy hat in a gallant gesture. "I told my assistants that we needed to get the sunrise in our camera shots, so they'll be going through the station for the perfect views. Are you one of the owners of the café?"

For a moment, her brain refused to work before she managed to stammer a welcome. "That's right. My name is Debbie Albright. We're so glad to have you at the Whistle Stop Café, Mr. Devons. Although we were expecting you later."

His tanned cheeks lifted with amusement. "Forgive me. My assistants, Jude Kipper and Victor Mortimer, tell me I can be a handful some days. Once I get an idea, I must see it through to the very end. The sunrise on the snow was spectacular. Have you ever driven out to see a winter sunrise? And you have a partner in this business, right?"

The abrupt subject change startled her, but she recovered. "Yes, her name is Janet Shaw. She's finishing up the baking in the kitchen. I'm sure she'll be out soon, but say the word if you want me to go and get her."

"I would never take her away from her work. Debbie and Janet." He tapped his temple. "I won't forget."

"There are some nice stained glass windows your cameraman might get a shot of," Debbie told him brightly. "They are original to the station. If you catch the sun at the right moment, they glow like jewels."

That was a bit more dramatic than she'd intended, but Maurice gestured for the cameraman as he stepped into the café. "Jude, Debbie says we should prioritize the stained glass windows," Maurice said. "Make it happen."

"Sure thing," the cameraman said as he struggled with the door and his camera bag. He glanced at Debbie. "Is Kim Smith around? I'd love to chat with her about the museum."

Maurice clapped a hand on the younger man's shoulder. "Jude is a natural storyteller with his equipment. I like to let him roam to get what he needs for the show. We hope to reach over two million viewers for the Christmas special—a glimpse of the old Americana, full of whimsy and nostalgia."

Suddenly, she felt faint. Two million viewers watching her and Janet? She braced herself against the curved glass display case, which would soon hold freshly baked treats, and forced herself to remember Jude's question so that she could answer it. "Um, Kim's not here at the moment. She'll probably arrive around eight, and she'll be thrilled to give you a tour of the station. The Pullman sleeper cars and museum displays are especially nice and decorated for Christmas."

Up close, Maurice's eyes sparkled an emerald green against his tanned skin. Truthfully, she preferred Greg's brilliant blue eyes and his casual demeanor, which never failed to put her at ease. In contrast, Maurice radiated intensity. Debbie suspected that being around him for extended periods of time might grow draining.

Maurice appraised her a moment longer than necessary, his slow smile catching her off guard. "Something tells me I'm really going to enjoy my stay in Dennison, Ohio, Debbie Albright."

"I'm glad to hear it." Debbie was about to duck into the kitchen to grab Janet when, to her delight, the brass bell above the door jingled with the arrival of a familiar lanky form.

"There's my favorite café owner," Greg Connor said with a grin.

Maurice stepped back, his expression suddenly neutral as he kept his gaze on Debbie. "We'll chat later when you're free." He motioned for Jude to join him. "Let's see if we can scout outside the station further." The men hurried out of the café.

Exhaling in relief, she focused on Greg, who wore a pair of rugged jeans and a black thermal shirt. The aviator jacket with the sherpa lining completed his simple yet attractive style.

She was one blessed woman.

"You're busy this morning," he said as he braced his hands on the counter.

"Maurice Devons came early. I wasn't expecting him until eleven. Janet's in a bit of a rush trying to decorate cookies, and I barely finished the decorations in time," she explained as she fussed with the greenery around the cash register.

"That's Maurice Devons? He's not what I expected." Greg frowned. "I heard a few women oohing and aahing over the posters Kim posted of him at the grocery store yesterday."

"You've never seen his videos online or the new TV series?" she asked as she fluffed one of the velvet bows tucked into the fragrant garland.

He raised a playful eyebrow. "I can't say I have. If he's got anything about renovations, I could be talked into watching it with you." As a contractor, Greg always kept abreast of his industry's best practices.

"Good to know. I'll save those episodes," she teased. "The coffee is ready, so we can grab you a cup before you head out the door."

He wrestled off the lid of his silver thermos and handed it to her. Their fingers brushed, and she smiled.

"The boys are excited about Christmas decorating, and I told them we would all share Christmas dinner together." His eyes, that delightful blue hue, brought a delicious shiver to her. "Think you can carve out time to get a tree with us, like last year?"

"I'd love to join you and the boys. I can hardly wait," she said, her voice suddenly husky as she handed back his filled thermos.

He leaned over and gave her a quick peck on the cheek. "Great. See you soon."

As she watched him leave the café, joy filled her. This Christmas was going to be the best holiday, and nothing would ruin it.

After the breakfast rush that morning, Peggy Lee crooned "Winter Weather" over the speakers while Ricky Carosi, owner of the local Italian restaurant, Buona Vita, entered. When Debbie had first moved to Dennison, he had helped her solve the series of vandalisms around town. He approached the counter with a wrapped package under one arm.

"I've brought the painting for the wall of Christmas art." He gestured toward the golden wall now covered with winter paintings, including a sample of an Amish quilt square and a few watercolor pieces from the local high school art teacher.

"Your contribution will be the pièce de résistance," Debbie told him. "I've heard Eileen and Kim gush over it for years. Thank you for trusting us with it. I know everyone will love it."

Eileen Palmer, Kim's mother and the former stationmaster, had always had a soft spot for Alberto Carosi, the uncle of her husband, Rafe, who fought as a marine during World War II.

Instead of handing the painting over, Ricky held it to his chest. "Do you have a moment, Debbie? I was hoping we could chat about the art."

Her interest piqued, she indicated a free table. "Sure. I'll take a break and bring us some peppermint mochas to enjoy while we chat."

It didn't take long to fill the mugs and pile the whipped cream on top. Chocolate sprinkles followed. Greg's mom, Paulette, had come in for her shift, freeing Debbie to visit.

Ricky sat, his expression far away as he gazed out the windows.

Debbie set the tray down carefully, then slid into the seat opposite him, smiling at her longtime family friend. "What can I do for you, Ricky?"

He unwrapped the package to reveal a thick gilt frame, its gold leaf winking in the winter light streaming from the curtained window.

"That frame is incredible," Debbie murmured.

"It's a painting that has been in my family for decades. I came not only to loan it for your Christmas art walk-through, but to see if I can get some answers."

"Sounds like this painting might have a story." Debbie rested her elbows on the table and leaned forward as Ricky carefully pulled out the painting and placed it reverently in front of her.

Mary gazed back at her, eyes bright with love and wisdom. In her arms, the infant Jesus nestled, fast asleep while the Christmas star limned them in silver. In the background, dark palms seemed to sway with an invisible breeze. The image took her breath away and seemed to radiate peace.

Yet Ricky's brow furrowed as he gazed at the canvas. "I confess its history has always confused me. My grandfather told us that his brother, Nico, shipped the painting all the way from Italy in 1943 without any explanation. When my grandfather wrote to friends in Rome, he discovered that Nico had disappeared after Mussolini returned to power and that the Allies had invaded Italy. I need to know what happened to my great-uncle. My grandfather hung this painting in the living room year-round, but sometimes at Christmas, he would stand in front of it and cry. He never did discover what happened to his brother after the war. But he also admitted that he and Nico hadn't spoken for many years before the painting arrived."

She ignored the steaming mocha beside her, the cream melting as the chocolate sprinkles sank deeper into the hot drink. "It's a beautiful piece. I've never seen anything quite like it."

"My great-uncle Nico could have been a master. He refused to leave Italy in the '30s when Mussolini came to power. I think he intended to keep creating with his fellow artists and to watch over his nonna. But my grandfather saw the danger of the Fascist party and escaped, while Nico refused to believe Mussolini would ever fall to such depths. Grandfather and Nico argued about it. Grandfather wanted to bring their nonna to America with him, but she refused. And of course, Nico backed her decision to stay, leaving my grandfather feeling betrayed."

"That's so sad, Ricky."

He pressed his lips together. "I think my grandfather gave up on Nico, and then one day, the painting arrived in Dennison, delayed with the mail. It languished in US customs for months before it reached Grandfather. He always feared something terrible had happened to Nico."

"That's possible," Debbie agreed slowly.

"Rafe, my uncle, always said the painting had to be a message for the family. My grandfather thought the idea was silly. But I can't help thinking I'm missing something."

She studied the painting and the gilt frame. Over the years, much of the gold leaf had worn thin at the edges. "I think there's a message here. It's of hope and redemption and the real meaning of Christmas, showing the ultimate gift of God's son. This is certainly a precious heirloom meant to be cherished. Could it be a peace offering between estranged family members?"

Ricky finally took a sip of his mocha, but his brow remained furrowed. "Maybe you're right. Maybe it was nothing more than a gift to atone for the years of resentment. Regardless, I need to know what happened to Uncle Nico. Was he a traitor to the Italian people, as my grandfather insisted? Why did my great-uncle go missing after the Allies liberated Rome? I need to know the truth."

Debbie met his gaze squarely. "I'll do whatever I can to help you find it."

CHAPTER THREE

Rome, Italy
December 1, 1943

The knock rattled the front door a second time, startling Nico. He set the paintbrush on the table. By now, evening had fallen, and he glimpsed his disheveled reflection in the black windowpanes. Who would bother him at such a late hour?

The doorknob rattled, and a woman's cry pierced him. He stumbled to his feet and hurried across the hardwood floor. After sliding the latch free, he opened the door a crack.

The hall was dimly lit, like his apartment, but he saw a brown lock of hair, a flash of a faded green dress, and a tan sweater.

"Please let me in, Nico." The voice was young and breathless. He would recognize it anywhere.

He flung open the door to see Sophia Giudice with one arm folded tightly across her middle while the other hand clutched a basket. She glanced over her shoulder, her eyes wide. Her dark hair was usually rolled into a neat bun, but currently several strands tumbled free. Her chest heaved as if she had flown up the narrow staircase leading to the flats on the second floor.

"What are you doing out at such an hour?" he asked, too dumbfounded to move.

She leaned forward. "I can't talk out here. Please let me in for a moment, and then I'll leave. I promise not to take up too much of your time."

He stepped aside.

Ducking her head, she brushed past him, the scent of vanilla clinging to her.

As he engaged the lock, he tried not to listen to the voice of alarm shouting in his head.

"Did you have a late delivery?" Immediately his mind conjured the image of her driving her father's truck alone into some dangerous situation, with a cake perched on the seat next to her.

She shook her head. "Can you close the drapes?"

Her question startled him, since he rarely bothered with such privacy, especially during the day when he needed all the light he could get to paint. Regardless, he obeyed, yanking the shabby fabric over the windows. But not before he saw a car ease slowly down the street. It gleamed black beneath the streetlamps and had no headlights shining.

He paused at the window a moment longer, his pulse racing.

She stood frozen by the door as if she were carved of stone.

He moved to the next window and drew the drapes, ignoring the puff of dust that followed. But from the small gap where the curtains didn't meet, he monitored the street.

The black car turned and took another narrow street, lined with shops and apartments. A sigh of relief escaped him as the sleek vehicle faded into the shadows.

"The polizia seem to be patrolling the area. Should I be worried?"

His question clearly rattled her. She blinked rapidly as she clutched her basket like a shield. "I hope not."

Misgiving took root in his heart. What exactly had happened this evening for her to draw the attention of the ruthless police?

Before he could question Sophia further, a man's shout and the sound of pounding boots from the flat beneath them sent a frisson of horror through him.

Without a second thought, Nico caught Sophia by the elbow and steered her past the dingy table and the tiny kitchen to a small closet with nothing more than a brown curtain covering it. He thrust aside the curtain and pushed her and her basket into the space just as a fist pounded on the door.

"Stay hidden," he said through clenched teeth.

"Nico?" She sounded so desperate and helpless, nothing like her usual spirited demeanor.

"I'll take care of it. Don't make a sound." He drew the curtain and whirled to face whatever was coming.

"Open up in there," an imperious baritone voice demanded. "Now!"

He took his time crossing the floor, praying all the while for a miracle, even if he didn't believe in them anymore. Whoever stood on the other side wasn't Captain Accardo. Nico had no idea if he would face an ally or a foe.

He unlocked his door a second time, only to see the imposing figure of the chief of the secret police. The man didn't wait for an invitation but promptly muscled his way into the cramped flat. Nico's stomach rolled as he recognized his former classmate, who had made life miserable for so many.

The years had been kind to Matteo Verga. At thirty-one years of age, he was every inch the perfect

Italian specimen Mussolini praised—physical prowess with the physique portrayed in ancient Roman sculptures, much like the murals Nico had painted.

Unlike the pompous captain who clicked his heels at the station, Matteo simply stood in the small kitchen. He glanced around the cramped quarters, his icy gaze sliding to the posters hanging on the wall and finally landing on Nico.

Nico forced himself to appear relaxed. "Do you need something? I was told I had another week before bringing in the new art."

Matteo's lip curled in an unpleasant sneer. "I'm searching for a criminal who ran down this street. She resembles our Sophia Giudice, with a slender build, green dress, and brown hair. I was wondering if you've seen anything."

The way Matteo said "our Sophia" ignited a spark in Nico's chest.

"Surely not Sophia. She is so busy with her father's bakery," Nico replied. "I've been painting recruitment posters for the party, as you can probably see. It's been a quiet evening, but you are welcome to search the apartment." Although his mouth was dry, Nico swept his hand to the tight spot where Sophia hid behind the curtain. "My cupboards are quite bare, but I might manage to make coffee for you."

Matteo barked a laugh as he glanced at the closet's flimsy curtain. "Coffee? You are paid well for your efforts, aren't you?"

Nico held his breath.

The secret police officer flicked a dismissive hand at the other men waiting outside in the hall. "Go check the other apartments. I doubt you'll find a woman here." He glared at Nico while gesturing to the posters hanging on the walls. "Nor will we prevent you from painting for Il Duce any longer. After all, it's the best someone like you can do for his country. You'd never last on the front lines."

The snide response he longed to give would prolong Matteo's presence within the cramped apartment and risk Sophia's discovery. But the insult still brought a heat to Nico's neck. How could he forget those early school years when Matteo so easily beat all their classmates in wrestling or running? Matteo had loved to shove him around, especially when Sophia watched on the outskirts with her girlfriends. She had never liked the brute, even then.

No, Nico could not let Matteo find her inside that closet. He gritted his teeth and willed the bully to leave.

Matteo moved toward the front door but paused before the Nativity painting. Despite the dim lighting in the flat, the rich colors glowed. Soft brushstrokes illuminated young Mary's face, her cheeks flushed with triumph as she stared back at the chief of secret police. Most paintings depicted a meek Mary gazing at her beloved son. But Nico had wanted the viewer to get the sense that Mary had a triumphant message for the world.

"Come, see the Messiah I hold in my arms," she seemed to say, even as her lips parted in wonder.

After hours of bold and blocky art, Nico had taken great pleasure in creating something realistic yet ethereal with rich golds and serene blues.

Matteo approached the painting, his black boots squeaking against the scuffed floor. For a long moment, he stared at the Madonna.

A huff—or an intake of breath—came from the curtain. Nico dared not glance at the closet. Sweat trickled down the back of his neck as he struggled to maintain his composure.

"Surely this isn't for our illustrious leader," Matteo growled as he reached out to touch the canvas. Then he dropped his gloved hand to his side.

No, the painting was solely for Nico. It remained his last link to whatever shreds of humanity remained within him.

"It's merely a Christmas piece. Nothing more." The answer sounded so pathetic and quiet after Nico's initial bravado that he tried not to flinch.

Yet the police chief appeared bothered by the small canvas. Matteo pivoted from the Madonna, his stare piercing Nico. "You were always weak, even as a boy. And I doubt she or anyone else would ever come to you for help, but if I find out you are lying..."

The threat hung in the air, along with the burning insults. Nico bowed his head as the chief of secret police brushed past him and out of the apartment.

CHAPTER FOUR

*A*fter Ricky left for his restaurant, Debbie hung the painting on the café wall. She stepped back to admire it. Contrasted with the yellow walls and vibrant crimsons and greenery, the brilliant blues and metallic neutrals drew plenty of attention.

In fact, a small group of customers gathered around the artwork, murmuring as Debbie straightened the frame one last time. Patricia Franklin, Harry Franklin's granddaughter, entered the café for her usual peppermint mocha before dashing to her law practice. She waved at Debbie and paused, her gaze snagging on the artwork.

"You have Ricky's painting? The one from Italy?" Patricia came to stand beside Debbie. A light dusting of snow melted on her forest-green coat and matching beret.

"The very one."

"It's stunning." Patricia studied it. "And it's just in time for the TV special."

Before Debbie could answer, a collective gasp echoed throughout the café as someone cried out, "Oh my goodness. It's Maurice Devons from *Days of Yesteryear.*"

Debbie turned to see Maurice with Kim, who blushed as she stopped at the café entrance while the guests mobbed them. Maurice tipped his cowboy hat with a charming grin and posed for a few selfies with the fans. He even signed autographs, winking at a few of the ladies.

"Oh boy, I've got to get an autograph." Patricia hurried to join the other women surrounding Maurice.

Debbie chuckled.

When Maurice caught her glance, his smile widened with a flash of impossibly white teeth. He really was a handsome man.

Not that it made any difference to her whether he was attractive. She and Greg shared something wonderful, a spark that had become several dates, not to mention a shared first kiss after he had rescued her from a crumbling church tower. It had been sweet and spontaneous, born from escaping danger, that had completely changed their relationship. Men like Greg didn't come around often, and she had no intention of letting him go.

Bemused, she faced the painting again, leaving Maurice to his avid fans.

Ricky's plea for her to discover what had happened to his great-uncle still resonated with her. She had solved several local cases, many with ties to World War II. Could she find what had happened to a man lost in Italy eighty years earlier?

Why had Nico sent the painting to his brother without explanation?

The question would have to wait. Janet likely needed Debbie's help in the kitchen, and soon the women clustering around the social media star would order hot drinks and Christmas cookies.

"Debbie Albright." Maurice's voice stopped her in her tracks. "I've been eager to chat with you—when you are free, that is. Should I wait until your customers are served?"

She was pleased that he was polite enough to realize that she had a business to run. "Would you like a mocha? I'm sure it won't take too long to fill the orders."

He nodded, his gaze lingering a little longer than she was used to. "My cameramen will be wandering through the station, planning the perfect shots. I won't be going anywhere for a while."

She ducked away to fill orders. She asked Paulette to deliver Maurice's mocha. When she looked up again, he stood by the painting, studying it as if deep in thought.

Paulette sidled up to Debbie. "I'll take over the counter. Our star wants to take the painting off the wall to get it appraised. I said no, but he's not listening to me."

Debbie glanced at the man, who stood as if at an art gallery while he slowly sipped from his cup.

"Thanks, Paulette. I'll take care of it." It was interesting that Maurice also seemed to be captivated by the painting. Could he help her discover more about Nico?

As if sensing her presence, Maurice spoke without taking his gaze from the painting. "Where did you find this piece?"

"Our friend Ricky Carosi, from the local Italian restaurant, loaned us this heirloom family painting for our Christmas celebration. We're hoping our tiny art gallery will bloom into a Christmas tradition for Dennison."

Maurice leaned forward, pulling out a pair of tortoiseshell glasses. "I'd like to learn more about the artist. What can you tell me?"

She retold some of Ricky's story, leaving out the part about the estranged brothers. "I'm also trying to find out what happened to

Nico Carosi. Apparently, he painted for the government in Italy during the Second World War and then disappeared."

"Are you familiar with the art movement in Italy during the 1930s and '40s?" Maurice asked.

She shook her head.

He blew out a slow breath as he put on his glasses. "So much art was stolen in those days. The Nazis and the Fascist party took whatever they wanted from families. Much of it was never relocated or returned. Famous and obscure masterpieces went missing, tucked into underground bunkers. Is this one of those stolen pieces, perhaps?"

Then, to her shock, he stretched out his long arms and snagged the painting off the wall, lowering it to one of the tables, which was thankfully clean.

"Please, I don't want it taken off the wall. And no, it can't be one of those confiscated pieces you described. Nico Carosi painted it."

Yet, as soon as the words left her mouth, a sliver of unease crept through her. Ricky had questions regarding Nico, including plenty of concerns. Perhaps she shouldn't be so quick to defend a man she knew nothing about. After all, to her knowledge, the Carosis merely assumed Nico had painted the piece. Nico had sent no explanation with it.

Maurice ignored her protest, pushing his glasses farther up his nose. "Do you see the markings on the painting?" He pointed to the star.

Despite her initial misgiving, her curiosity took over. There in the night sky lay a series of letters, so subtle that they might simply have been intentional color fluctuations to add depth. Debbie had noticed the details of a mouse darting into the shadows, the starlight glimmering above with streams of silver moonlight, and the rough spun folds of Mary's tunic, but she hadn't noticed the letters.

"It's Latin," Maurice said, his voice a low murmur. "Our artist wrote in Latin. *Ecce ad astrum.*"

"What does it mean?" Debbie asked as she studied the delicate letters.

Maurice shot her a side glance. "'Behold the star.' I only know because my mother taught me Latin as a child. Who knew it would come in handy with antiques?" His gaze narrowed as his long, tanned fingers hovered over the gilt frame. "It's loose."

She had been so careful when she'd hung it. Surely she hadn't broken it. Ricky would have taken the utmost care with it as well. On the other hand, Maurice had grabbed it before she could intervene.

The frame had shifted a centimeter or so, revealing a slip of frayed canvas. Debbie frowned. Ricky would be displeased to see his painting damaged.

"I would like to take the painting to study it, and I can have the frame fixed as well." Maurice reached out as if to grab it again, but Debbie placed a staying hand on his arm. His eyes widened a fraction at her touch.

She withdrew her hand quickly, her face heating, mostly with ire at his increasingly presumptuous behavior. "I must speak with the painting's owner first, as it is still his property and merely on loan to us. I don't have the authority to give you permission to take it anywhere. I'm sure you understand. Until Ricky says so, the painting must remain here."

Maurice's dark eyebrows dipped downward. All at once, she saw the oozing charm harden into something quite unpleasant.

"Debbie, I am an expert in antiques, and I have contacts who can help on the rare occasion I'm stumped. Call your friend and let him know that Maurice Devons wants to feature his painting on *Days of Yesteryear*."

She frowned at the imperious command as she pulled out her phone and typed a text to Ricky, explaining the situation and asking if he was okay with Maurice's involvement.

Ricky's answer came seconds later. No. I DON'T WANT THE PAINTING TO LEAVE THE CAFÉ. THAT FRAME HAS ALWAYS BEEN A LITTLE LOOSE. NOT TO WORRY, DEBBIE. I'LL FIX IT WHEN I GET OFF WORK.

But when she relayed Ricky's answer, Maurice's neck reddened. "Did you tell your friend that I will take care of it? I have a framer who specializes in restoring antique canvases."

She shook her head. "You're welcome to speak with Ricky yourself, but this is as far as I can go with this discussion. You might catch him at his restaurant."

"I don't think you understand. My show is about treasures." He gestured to the Madonna and Christ child. "This is something very, very special. I can feel it. And my instincts are never wrong."

Kim joined them. "Why don't we finish the tour of the museum, Mr. Devons?" She cast a knowing glance in Debbie's direction, as if to say she had overheard plenty of the conversation. "I've got several collections I'd love to show you and your camera crew, including the railcars. You can have exclusive filming with no interruptions. Did you know that back during World War II, the canteen made doughnuts famous? I've even got a sandwich bag from 1943 kept under glass."

Maurice straightened his bolo necktie with a jerk. "I demand to study that painting as I see fit, or there won't be a show. It's the painting or nothing." He pivoted on his heel and motioned to his crew.

"Now, Mr. Devons, do be reasonable," Kim protested as she hurried to catch up with the online celebrity who stormed out of the café, leaving a powerful trail of cologne in his wake. "Surely we can come to some kind of agreement, as the painting doesn't belong to anyone in the building."

Debbie recoiled at the idea of so much drama playing out before the guests, some who watched with mouths agape. She took the painting to the office for safekeeping until Ricky could fix the frame. Though she smiled and offered to refill coffee for the customers, her cheeks burned at the memory of Maurice's behavior.

Retreating to the kitchen, she found Janet ladling fragrant tortellini soup laced with rosemary into a pair of bowls, with steaming rolls on the accompanying plates.

"Janet, our star has threatened to cancel the show if he can't have Ricky's painting."

Janet froze with the dripping ladle in midair. "But we've worked so hard to get him here. If he cancels, we may not get as big a draw as we hoped."

"We've got plenty to offer, with or without a huffy star," Debbie soothed as she tightened the strings of her apron. "Kim might be able to calm him down, but he actually had the nerve to pull the painting off the wall without asking permission first. Regardless, Ricky wants it on the café wall. There it will remain unless Ricky permits otherwise."

Janet returned to the pot of soup and topped off the nearest bowl with a few extra tortellini. "I hope so. I always thought Maurice was so charming on his show."

"Real life doesn't seem to match the glittering persona. Regardless, we will persist in our holiday plans." Debbie waited for her friend to set the ladle on a spoon rest and then slid an arm around Janet's shoulders. "We are going to have the best Christmas yet, you'll see. We've got each other. We have family."

"And Greg," Janet teased. "Don't forget him."

Debbie grinned in return as the memory of him filled her mind. She still couldn't believe she'd be sharing her Christmas with Dennison's best renovation specialist. She had grown to love his quiet, steady demeanor and sense of humor. Life was good. Who needed a diva to put the café on the map?

"I'll see what's going on outside the café. I'm sure Kim will smooth things over."

But as Debbie left the kitchen, she saw the entire TV crew exiting the café with mochas in hand. One cameraman shot her an apologetic look, shrugging one shoulder as he pushed open the door to leave. Through the nearest window, Debbie saw Kim outside, gesturing widely while Maurice lowered the brim of his Stetson hat. He gave the impression of a bull about to charge. His aide, the blond Jude, reached out to touch Maurice's arm, but the star continued to glower.

"Oh boy," Debbie murmured as she headed past the tables.

Surely one sulky star couldn't ruin their plans. Could he?

CHAPTER FIVE

Nico waited for a full minute after the police left, fighting the urge to dash to the windows to see which direction Matteo headed. He dared not get Sophia out of the closet for fear the secret police would return. The sound of cars rumbling down the street brought him no peace. When he finally peered around the drapes, he saw no retreating taillights or men stalking the streets.

But he wasn't a fool. Matteo would watch the street all night long with guards posted in the alleys and tucked in doorways. Worse, desperate families offered to watch the neighborhoods for unusual behavior, reporting even innocent actions, all in exchange for the privilege of extra bread rations. In September, the city had been torn apart by the resistenza known as the Partisans. Those loyal to the Fascist party vowed to never let it happen again.

Nico let the drape ease back into place. More minutes passed, and not a sound from Sophia. Clearly she also feared a return.

Finally, when the minute hand of the clock inched twenty minutes past nine o'clock, Nico moved toward the curtain of the closet and reached for her.

She grasped his hand tightly, her fingers cold to the touch. When he led her out of the dank space littered with oil paints, a bottle of turpentine to clean his brushes, and a stack of canvases, she swayed, tipping forward as if she might faint. Without thinking, he grasped her elbow, offering to steady her.

"Matteo spoke your name," he said.

"Yes. I heard," she whispered, her dark eyes searching his, as if to read his thoughts.

The answer gave Nico nothing to work with.

He pulled out one of the chairs at the table and gestured for her to sit. Silently, she obeyed, her back straight and prim, though her fingers shook as she folded her hands. The table was littered with the tools of his trade, the wood stained from various oil paints.

He waited, hoping she would tell him why she had landed on his doorstep of all places and why the chief of the secret police hunted her. But the silence within the flat was interrupted by nothing but the ticking of the clock on the wall—and the soft hum of a car's motor outside.

They both glanced at the window at the same time. A shudder rippled through her when she faced him again.

He realized that if he wanted specific questions answered, he would have to ask them outright. "Please, Sophia. I need to know why you came to me tonight. And why does Matteo search for you?"

Sophia took a deep, shuddering breath. "Tonight, I delivered a special order to one of the hospitals. Papa feels so poorly these days. The delivery took longer than I thought it would, as our truck often stalls. Unfortunately, I had to leave it at the Fatebenefratelli Hospital and walk this evening. I never meant to exceed the curfew. When I heard one of the police shout, I ran." She patted a trembling hand over her hair to smooth the stray locks. She avoided his gaze for the briefest second, but it was enough to cast doubt in him. An evening bakery order to one of the local hospitals?

And to the Fatebenefratelli Hospital, which housed men and women ill with the mysterious Syndrome K, a highly contagious neurological disease that came with terrifying symptoms and eventually death?

Nico shook his head. "I don't like it. Matteo won't stop until he finds you. He seems to think you are guilty of more than delivering baked goods."

"He has no reason not to trust me. I deliver bread in this area of the city, even to his men. Besides, he didn't see my face tonight. He can't prove that he saw me do anything illegal."

"Yet here you are."

"Here I am." Her eyes widened at the garish posters demanding full allegiance to Mussolini. Perhaps, in her desperate haste, she had not noticed them when she had first entered Nico's apartment. "I did not realize you painted for Mussolini."

He heard the quiet dread in her tone. Over the past few years, he had thought it best to keep his art activities quiet. Considering how much she and many others hated the police, he had all but hidden his work on the posters, preferring anonymity after the newspapers published effusive praise of his enormous murals. He had painted them with a team of fellow artists, but he told no one, wished for no fame or recognition.

Instead, he felt only shame, for the art told a lie. Worse, it was wicked.

"I had no choice. I was recruited in the early days, but then everything changed once the party came into full power," he told her.

He remembered the terrible threats leveled against his grandmother should he rebel. But ever since he had taken the brush on Il Duce's behalf, Nico's reputation lay in tatters. Frustrated at trying to explain his past failures, he instead shoved a hand through his hair. No one refused Mussolini and walked away to tell the tale.

"Will you turn me in?" Her voice was small in the hush of the apartment as she placed her basket on the ground. She gestured to the garish art. "After all, you work for them."

He dropped his hand, his chest throbbing at the idea of ratting out Sophia Giudice to a man such as Matteo. Or the pompous captain who pretended to be a critic of the fine arts.

"Never." Nico stared at her, willing her to see his sincerity. Yet, his gaze dropped to her basket all the same. The contents within had shifted in haste. A white slip of paper peeked out between the precious loaves of bread. "I am not one of them, Sophia, even if I design the posters. You have always been my friend, and I hope that will never change. But I am not a fool either. You do more than deliver goods, yes?" He reached down and plucked out the message. He held it out to her, as if daring her to take it.

For a long moment, she remained silent. Then she cleared her throat and accepted the slip of paper. She

45

folded it and slipped it into her pocket. "I pass the occasional message when I deliver baked goods."

For the resistenza? If she expected him to be surprised, she would be sorely disappointed. Such news hardly shocked him, especially when he remembered her standing up to Matteo years ago when they had attended the local school.

When Matteo had pushed Nico off his bike with the intent to steal it, Sophia had planted herself firmly on the cobblestone street with her fists propped on her hips. At twelve years of age, she had towered over Nico and everyone else, except Matteo. The tongue-lashing she had delivered had been legendary in the neighborhood for months afterward. Sophia had become Nico's savior that day. Was it any wonder that she would endanger herself now as a grown woman?

"I will go now. I dare not get you into trouble." She began to rise from the table.

Nico caught her wrist and tugged her back down into the rickety chair. "No. The street will be watched. It's too dangerous for you."

A strangled laugh escaped her as she tried to fix her lopsided chignon. "I can't stay in your flat."

He bit the inside of his cheek until it throbbed. "You must. You can sleep on the bed, and I'll stay up on the couch and watch in case someone returns. But the moment you leave here, we'll both be in trouble, as will your contacts. Captain Accardo has orders to sweep the city. I heard as much earlier today. Matteo will not stop searching."

Her eyes glittered in the flickering lamplight before she dashed away a stray tear with her fist. "You don't understand, Nico. I must deliver the message as soon as possible."

He held his tongue. Sometimes when he chose silence, men and women filled in the gap with nervous chatter, giving him far more information than he would have known to ask for. He would never betray Sophia, but he wanted to know the full extent of her predicament.

"I must." She leaned forward, her eyes round. "If I don't, people will die."

"If you do, you will die. The streets are crowded with SS officers, especially since the Nazis freed Mussolini from his captivity. Moreover, rumors abound of the Allies infiltrating northern Italy and lower Sicily as we speak."

"I know. I have limited time to leave Rome before everything falls apart."

Her resolved answer chilled him to the bone. "You want to leave Rome?"

"I've got to warn the resistenza north of the city. We also have an opportunity to enlist the help of the

Allies as they invade Rome from the north. To let them know who they can trust and who they can't. Innocents will be caught in the crossfire if we do nothing. We must protect the helpless at all costs."

Nico blew out a harsh breath as he shifted on the hard chair. If she went—and he knew she would—she would encounter danger at every turn, with plenty of checkpoints manned by SS and Italian soldiers. Any Allies who made it past the German defenses near the coast would be forced to cross the dreaded Winter Line, a series of three guarded lines designed to defend a western section of Italy, including the town of Monte Cassino. From Monte Cassino, the highway ran unin- terrupted to Rome. There was no telling which Allied army would reach Rome first.

But he had bigger problems to worry about.

No one would be able to leave the city without attract- ing the attention of the Nazis. The Germans used their presence in the country to pull the Jews from their homes, moving them into the camps. The Italians had their own camps too. If the Allies did infiltrate as deep as Rome, the city would be rife with war and power struggles. Not even the sacred season of Christmas would bring peace.

"It's madness. Why must you go?"

Her throat bobbed with effort. "I have many rea- sons, some of which I can't share. But I will tell you what I can. My brother remains up north with the *resistenza*. I must find him and deliver a message." A tear slid down her cheek. Nico longed to wipe it away, but he merely folded his hands.

Her brother was two years older than Nico and Sophia. Rumor had it that Paolo Giudice had run away from home. His absence at the bakery remained a mystery, and Sophia had taken over many of her brother's duties.

"Does your papa know of your activities?"

She shook her head. "Papa is much like you. He wants peace, not war. He willingly serves the secret police plenty of pastries and whatever else they demand, claiming that it will keep all of us safe. I cannot argue with him. It is better that he doesn't know about Paolo's role or mine." Then her voice dropped to a whisper. "I don't know if Paolo is even alive. Few would care, it seems."

The pain inside Nico's chest intensified. Was that how she saw him, as someone who stood on the sidelines, refusing to do anything? The idea stung him. He had done everything he could to keep his grandmother safe. He could understand Sophia's desire to protect her brother.

Nico rose and headed toward his cupboard, needing to work out some of the restlessness that had built up inside him. "You must be hungry. At least rest for a *while and have a cup of coffee or tea before you go." He found a plate of dried biscotti, a kettle, and two chipped mugs, then lit the stove.*

She offered him a trembling smile. "Tea would be nice."

Painting for the government brought certain perks during the season of rations, and he retrieved the dented tea canister. Before long, the kettle whistled. He brought a tray of biscotti, cheese, and olives to the table. When he came back with the tea, her fingers brushed against his as she accepted her cup. A spark lit all the way through his veins, and he quickly ducked his head.

He couldn't allow his emotions to show, yet he felt the sharp stab of fear. For her and for himself.

Sophia had always been stubborn. Fearless. But fearlessness could translate to recklessness.

They ate in silence, his mind whirling and her pale brow pinched as she studied the week-old biscotti before dunking it into her tea and taking a cautious nibble.

"Do you have transport out of the city?" he finally asked.

"Yes. A farmer offered to meet me at the ancient Forum. I'll get a ride in his truck and head northeast to—" She abruptly cut herself off before revealing her brother's location. She gestured to his Nativity painting. "I've never seen anything so lovely. Who is it for?"

"I don't know. I just felt compelled to create it."

Years ago, he had thought his faith entirely lost, trampled beneath the thundering march of countless black boots hitting the pavement and the cries of the party demanding total, unquestioning obedience. Who could stand against such monstrosity? Who could fight the will of the Tiber River carving through the heart of Rome? The party rushed onward through Italy with the same unrelenting power, sweeping away everything in its path.

He was just one man—an artist at that, not a soldier.

Yet it was strange that at Christmas he should think of the Christ child hiding from Roman conquerors and the jealous Herod. Joseph had taken his wife and Jesus under the cover of night, escaping the wrath of soldiers to head to Egypt—an act of resistance, if there ever was one.

When Sophia sank into a weary slumber on the couch, Nico took the night watch even as his eyes burned with fatigue. He made another pot of tea and sank deep into thought as he returned to the window overlooking the street. The night remained quiet, with no stars to illuminate the darkness and the street below eerily empty.

He stared at the painting and the frame lying beside it—the wood thick and carved, brushed with a thin layer of gold paint. Then he studied the woman lying beneath a blanket on the couch, her face softened in sleep, reminding him of the young girl who had defied Matteo all those years ago to protect Nico. She would defy even Mussolini, if given the chance.

He would not see harm come to her. Resolve hardened within him as he took the painting from the easel, the paint dry enough to handle, though the heavy scent of oil and turpentine lingered.

His gaze landed on the ornate frame. And suddenly, an idea exploded within him, stealing his breath.

Rummaging in his paint box, he found a knife perfect for carving wood. As the clock ticked to a steady rhythm, he worked through the night.

CHAPTER SIX

*S*aturday morning, Debbie checked the tables while she served guests coffee. Paulette worked the register, waiting on a line of customers who wanted treats. Janet had baked cherry tarts and Scottish shortbread, which proved exceptionally popular. Apparently, Janet's husband, Ian, had bragged to the police department and the school board about his wife's melt-in-your-mouth cookies.

Janet couldn't have appeared more pleased with the extra orders, clearly living her baking dream as she bustled around the kitchen. Debbie loved seeing her dear friend in her element while slicing the rows of buttery shortbread.

The bell over the door sounded, and Maurice's assistants, Jude and Victor, entered the café.

She waved at them in welcome before turning her attention to a young mother with a toddler. As she poured coffee for the mother, she overheard Jude ordering doughnuts.

"Can't beat these doughnuts in Dennison," he said. "I've never had anything quite so good. If I gain weight this Christmas, I'm blaming the Whistle Stop Café."

"You could use a little more meat on your bones for these cold Ohio winters," Paulette told him merrily.

As Debbie approached the counter to refill her pot, she noticed Jude and Victor had stopped at the newly repaired painting on the wall. They spoke in low voices, and she couldn't hear what they said.

After a moment, Jude caught her gaze and waved. "We'll be back for coffee later."

"Glad to hear it," she called. "Come in anytime."

Later that afternoon, after a rush of customers, Paulette put together a pot of coffee and a tray of mugs for the volunteers in the Nativity play on the train. When the last restaurant guests left, Debbie watched as several cars pulled up to the café entrance. She spotted Ricky, who would be playing a wise man, and Liza Quincy, who would play the role of Mary, hurrying up to the café door.

Debbie beat them to the door and propped it open.

"Brrr." Ricky rubbed his hands together when he entered. "It's brisk out there today."

"There's fresh coffee waiting for you, and dessert," Debbie told him.

Liza smiled a greeting, which was extra charming because of the cute fur earmuffs she wore. Liza worked full-time at the local grocery store while she figured out what she wanted to study in college. She was taking general education courses that would be able to transfer to most programs when she chose a path.

"Hey, kiddo, did you know Tiffany will be home for Christmas?" Debbie asked. Janet's daughter, Tiffany Shaw, was in her second year at Case Western Reserve University. She and Liza had been friends in high school.

Liza pulled off her muffs and ran her fingers through her hair. "We plan to meet for coffee when she arrives the week of Christmas."

Another young man entered the café, wearing a black parka.

Liza greeted him brightly. "Brad Croft? It's been a while. How are you doing?"

He grinned, his cheeks bright pink. That might have been due to the cold, but Debbie suspected otherwise when she saw how he looked at Liza. "Hi, Liza. It feels like forever, even if we did graduate from high school together."

"Brad volunteered to help with the Nativity. He's going to wrangle our ornery donkey and sheep, and he'll even play a wise man on the train," Debbie explained to Liza.

"That's great. Is your dad still farming?" Liza asked, falling into step with him.

"Still farming. I help him when I can—although..."

Debbie paused when she heard a strangled cough from Brad. Ricky glanced at her and Brad, his face settling into a careful, neutral expression.

Brad stumbled but then carried on as if nothing had happened. "I'm thinking about taking a chef's course. I want to cook more than farm."

"That's awesome. You have so many options with culinary schools," the young woman effused as she unwound her crimson scarf. The two sat at a table, where Paulette poured them coffee.

"Who else is volunteering for the play?" Ricky asked as he checked his watch.

"Ian's sick, so he needs to rest, which means we'll need to replace him as wise man. Harry plans on coming. I'll probably suggest that he take over for Brad as a wise man so that Brad can be Joseph," Debbie said. "Of course, you'll be another wise man, along with Janet's dad."

Ricky nodded absently as he shoved his hands into his coat pockets.

"Have you heard from Maurice Devons with *Days of Yesteryear*?" Debbie asked as she headed toward the table. She sat with the other cast members.

A small sigh escaped Ricky as he sat beside Debbie. "Yes I have, as a matter of fact. I had the privilege of receiving several imperious calls, demanding I hand over my painting for quite an impressive price. The last offer ended with a 'Do you know who I am?'"

Debbie groaned. "He didn't."

A twinkle appeared in Ricky's eyes. "You'll be happy to know that I chose not to respond. I've got too much to do to waste time sparring with the host of *Days of Yesteryear*. The money is tempting, but I can't part with our family painting. However, I am curious why Maurice would be so interested."

"Perhaps your great-uncle deserves a bit of acclaim. I've had guests commenting on the Nativity painting all day, some even asking if the artist is local. It makes me wonder if Maurice might help us with the history if he wasn't so pushy," Debbie said.

Ricky chewed on his bottom lip. He eyed the Madonna and child hanging on the far wall. "My cousin Leo would know more about the history."

"Can we ask him?"

Ricky shook his head, his expression suddenly shuttered. "No, we can't ask Leo." His tone sounded final. "It's a shame the rhinestone cowboy canceled the show over my painting. I'm sorry, Debbie."

Debbie wanted to ask more, but the bell above the entrance tinkled as Janet's father, Steve Hill, pushed open the door. He shook off the snow dusted on his head and grinned when he saw Debbie. "Hello, Debbie. Will my dear daughter be joining us?"

"As soon as she finishes a few things in the kitchen."

Steve joined the merry band around the table.

Kim and her husband, Barry, entered the café, Kim's cheer a little more subdued than usual. Harry followed with his dog, Crosby, and greeted everyone warmly as he pulled a chair to the table. Crosby sank down at his master's feet with his great tongue lolling.

"Still no word on Maurice?" Debbie asked Kim.

Kim shrugged out of her wool coat and slung it over one of the tables. "No. He's not answering my phone calls. I'm absolutely devastated by this turn of events. We all worked so hard to make this holiday extra special. Who cancels a Christmas show?"

Debbie wrapped an arm around Kim. "We'll have a live Nativity and a special train ride. It will be wonderful for the families to hear a reading of the Nativity and ride through the country while the snow falls. Our festivities will be beautiful."

Janet ducked out of the kitchen and added, "We'll make it work. I'm planning plenty of hot cocoa for the guests, along with Christmas cookies. Something easy to hold in mittened hands. And the animals will be so cute."

"The donkey can be a handful, but he loves being around kids," Brad chimed in from the table. "They can pet him and the sheep. We'll put a fenced area outside in the parking lot, and people can come and go as they please."

Everyone started sharing their excitement, and soon any discussion of the social media star disappeared.

Barry glanced around the room. "I must say, the café is very festive." He frowned after a moment, his gaze pinned to the ceiling. "Is it me, or is your security camera angled differently?"

Debbie looked at the camera perched high on the wall. It was angled away from the doors.

Kim shook her head. "Isn't that the way it's usually positioned?"

"No." Barry folded his arms across his chest. "I've got a good memory."

Kim chuckled while shaking her head. "You have such an imagination, Barry."

"Sweetie, I am *not* kidding about the camera. I notice these things," Barry protested.

Kim shook her head, but her cheeks dimpled regardless.

Barry and Kim had the cutest relationship, and their little marital disagreement drew a few grins from the others sitting near enough to overhear the debate. Neither Kim nor Barry worried about speaking their mind to each other. Debbie loved how Barry reached for Kim's hand even after he made the point about the camera. Ever tender, Barry made Debbie think of Greg. How lovely would it be to have such a comfortable, safe relationship that lasted over the years? To be married that long and still genuinely enjoy each other?

"It probably makes me a bad business owner, but I can't remember how they are usually positioned," Debbie admitted as she glanced up at the ceiling. She hadn't paid the camera much attention in the past months. When Ian was better, she might ask him about it. For now, she would focus on the play.

The reading went smoothly since everyone had worked on memorizing their lines at home. Now, working together, they shared plenty of smiles. Although she didn't miss how Brad and Ricky seemed to avoid each other, their gazes never quite meeting.

Kim's phone chimed. She pulled it out of her purse and frowned.

"What is it, Kim?" Debbie asked.

"Our train engineer, Taylor Haverly, called in sick. Can you believe it? He has the stomach flu and went to the hospital where he was diagnosed with dehydration. Apparently, he also has walking pneumonia on top of it all," Kim said. "I mean, he's usually very healthy, so he'll probably make a full recovery, but he'll definitely be out of commission for a while."

"He'll be in our prayers," Debbie said, and the others murmured agreement.

"What will we do about the train?" Janet wondered aloud. "Who can operate it on such short notice, especially during this season?"

Debbie folded her arms across her chest. The Christmas festivities were rapidly unraveling, and she couldn't put them all back together. Her picture-perfect moment had evaporated faster than the steam of a lukewarm latte.

Kim's face lit up. "I think I know who we can call. Leo Carosi used to run the train years ago. Why don't we see if he'd be willing to come out of retirement until Taylor is back on his feet? He lives near Sugarcreek, which is quite close. Do you think he'd go for it, Ricky?"

A strangled sound escaped Ricky, and he paled despite the excited chatter around him from the other volunteers. Abruptly, he shot to his feet. "I've got to get to the restaurant for the supper rush. Good night, everyone. Great acting from each of you." He waved at Janet. "Thanks again for the treats."

Without another word, he snatched his coat, thrusting his arms into the sleeves as he marched out the exit.

"Ricky seems upset," Brad commented mildly.

Debbie checked the time. "It's nearly five thirty. I suppose we ought to wrap things up. Who will call Leo?"

Kim grabbed her coat as everyone rose to leave. Faint lines around her eyes crinkled as she tried to smile and failed. "I will, but I had hoped Ricky would volunteer to, being family and all. It appears that I will be the one to coax Leo out of retirement *and* extend the olive branch to our illustrious, pouting star, Mr. Devons."

"Star? More like diva," Barry said, sounding unimpressed. He held the café door open for his wife, glancing up as she strolled through. "I still say the camera was changed."

Kim's laughter floated down the hall. "Thanks, honey. I needed that."

Debbie ran over the details of Ricky's behavior as she and Janet ran through the closing tasks for the café. Ricky had shot down her suggestion of asking Leo about the painting, then the idea of his cousin filling in as train engineer. Why? Was there bad blood between the cousins?

As she polished the glass display case while Paulette cleaned the coffeepot and a subdued Janet left the café, Debbie sincerely hoped that Christmas wouldn't be ruined for everyone.

CHAPTER SEVEN

Rome, Italy
December 2, 1943

A hand touched Nico's cheek, then brushed the hair from his forehead, while a sweet voice murmured for him to wake up. But Nonna and his mother were gone, and his family no longer remained in Rome. He blinked several times and found Sophia standing near him with her lips quirked up at the corners. She drew the blanket around her shoulders as morning light seeped through the faded curtains.

For a moment, he struggled to regain his bearings. What was Sophia doing in his apartment? He, being a gentleman, would never allow a woman to stay so long, yet the police—Matteo—had made it impossible for her to leave.

He straightened in the chair, rubbing the crick in his neck, then his back. A sense of urgency flared in him, making his pulse race as he remembered the secret police searching the city for dissidents.

"You fell asleep working on that, didn't you?" she asked, a tint of humor coloring her voice.

He glanced at the Nativity canvas, flat on the table with the frame mostly assembled, shavings of wood curled beside it.

She didn't seem to be examining his work, which had taken most of the night, her dark gaze trained on him. "Or were you keeping watch?" she asked softly, serious once more.

He fidgeted with a sleeve that had come loose and fallen over his wrist, lest he betray the fear roiling within him. "I thought it best to stay awake."

Had she touched his face while he slept? Or was it some dream—one better banished to the recess of his mind?

"I'll make you coffee. Or tea," she said. "You need something better than stale biscotti. Something more nourishing."

He wanted to protest that it was her biscotti, but merely pressed his lips together. As she rustled for kindling and matches to light the stove, his blanket dragging on the ground and her stocking feet making no sound, it hit him how cold the apartment had become during the long night. She deserved better.

She folded the blanket and laid it on the couch. "No one came back?" She sounded hopeful.

"No one." He rose from the chair and peered out the window, his shoulders relaxing when he didn't see any unusual cars or black uniforms. Perhaps Matteo had directed his attention elsewhere. A few flakes of snow swirled down while the sky above remained a chilled gray.

Shivering, Nico returned to the safety of the kitchen, relieved to see the merry flames inside the pot-belly stove before she shut the door. Humming softly, Sophia grabbed a frying pan and found a few eggs. The crack of the shells, the hiss of the eggs hitting the iron pan, and the whistle of the kettle brought a curious warmth to his heart. How sweet and somehow right to have her in his kitchen. He could almost forget there was a war encroaching on his doorstep, with the Nazis determined to crush the invading Allies. His kitchen felt like home, the way it had when Nonna had cooked for him at Christmas.

He could almost imagine that he was nothing more than a simple artist, and that Sophia was his—

He shut down the thought as soon as it flitted across his mind. She would never tie herself to someone like him, and she shouldn't. He didn't deserve her.

Yet the idea of family at Christmas, of sharing it with someone special stayed with him, no matter how hard he chided himself.

"If the roads are clear, I'll leave," she told him over her shoulder. "There's no sense in prolonging the wait any longer. The sooner I can leave Rome, the better."

"What is the message you need to deliver?" he asked, folding his arms across his chest.

She pressed her lips together as the sounds of the eggs frying in the pan filled the silence. Then she squared her shoulders. "It's best if you don't ask too many questions. But I will tell you this—the tide is about to turn. We can end this war and take our country back. Il Duce is weakened."

"He's dangerous, Sophia. And he has the help of the Germans."

"But we might yet garner the help of the Allies. They press ever closer." She waved her wooden spoon, her eyes glowing like fire. "We almost had the city mere months ago. The Partisans would have won if only—"

He cut her off. "But they didn't win, and now you will endanger yourself."

She peered at him. "I have not heard from Paolo, and he always reaches out to me. Based on the last communication between us, he relied on the good graces of a nearby farmer to feed them. The rebels were nearly destitute then, and their radio went out two weeks ago. I have no choice. I must find my brother."

How could he argue with that? Would he not do the same if it were his own beloved brother in danger?

The smell of burnt eggs filled the room, and she hurried to scrape them from the frying pan. "I've ruined breakfast. I'm so sorry." Her voice broke as she pressed a fist against her mouth, no doubt thinking food was scarce enough as it was without carelessly ruining such a luxury as eggs.

But he wasn't concerned about breakfast. He was concerned about her. "Sophia, listen to me. I'll take the message. I won't read it. It's probably better if I don't. But I can carry it in my Nativity frame."

"You?" She gasped as she set the wooden spoon on the counter.

"I thought about it all night." As he spoke, he reached for the nearest propaganda poster and gently freed it of the pins. "And I've got the perfect alibi to slip past the Nazi checkpoints."

After eating burnt yet somehow delicious eggs with her, he drained the last of his tepid coffee before packing up each and every propaganda poster in the apartment. A thrill of excitement surged through him, tempered with dread. He hoped no one would question him as he traveled through checkpoints with the painting. If stopped, he'd merely wave a sample poster and hand it over, claiming he had a mission to plant posters in the nearest city or village along the way. If they asked about the small Nativity painting, he'd claim it had been purchased by a patron.

Sophia remained so silent after breakfast that he feared she might regret her decision to confide in him.

"I know I don't deserve your trust, but I will never betray you," he assured her. "Do you think you should return to the bakery? Matteo would have nothing against you or your father. It might be the best way."

"No," she said thickly. "I can't go back."

"Then stay with my neighbor, at least until the coast is clear."

Finally, she nodded. Sophia told him nothing about the message as she carefully folded it. To his surprise, she pulled out several large bills. With deft fingers, she folded them, making them as small as she could before handing them to him. Then she watched him with those large eyes as he carefully inserted the slip and money into the carved hollow of the frame. He chose the portion right above the star.

His eye caught on the star. The story of the wise men's journey resonated deep within him. Right now, he couldn't linger too much on such thoughts. What was he searching the stars for exactly? Redemption? Freedom? Forgiveness? A bitter laugh nearly broke free of him. For so long he had played it safe, hoping the chaos of the world wouldn't touch him. That somehow, he could ride out the war. Now, it had landed on his very doorstep. Alberto's warnings rippled through his mind. Someday you'll have to make a choice, and it will cost you. But what will you pay if you do nothing?

Guilt and shame warred within Nico—an all-too-familiar struggle.

He busied himself by nailing the frame together while the Madonna regarded him with something almost akin to joy. Even though he had painted her expression, it felt as if the figure had merely guided his brush.

Come, *she seemed to say.* Come and find the Messiah.

Next, he rolled several posters carefully and tied them with twine. He planned to take the promised offering to the pompous captain to dispel the suspicions of spies who might follow him. If all went well, he could escape Rome before noon.

He found extra blank papers and a few pencils to add to the bundle, giving instructions to Sophia as he worked.

"As soon as I leave, you should hide with my neighbor, Mia Ginerva. She's older and very sweet. You will be safe with her. She'll walk with you wherever you need to go."

His neighbor was nearly the same age as his nonna. Mia Ginerva wouldn't leave Rome for any reason, just as his nonna had so stubbornly refused to leave. So Nico had waited, hoping that everything he witnessed would blow over. It hadn't. Instead, he had found himself caught in a terrible web. His eyes watered as he tied a string around one stubborn picture that wouldn't stay rolled.

"I can't let you try to find my brother without my help," Sophia suddenly cried as he retrieved the last of the posters from the wall.

He placed a hand on her shoulder. "I'll find Paolo. How hard can it be?" He kept his tone light, knowing full well it would be difficult.

"He's in the mountains of Brisighella." She folded her arms across her chest, her expression bleak. "Or he was."

"I can find him in the mountains," Nico told her. It was a bold promise, and maybe one that would require a miracle, yet it fell from his lips easily.

"But he doesn't like you."

Nico's cheeks heated, and he resumed the task of stuffing posters into his worn leather satchel. "I can imagine. Nevertheless, I still believe it would be safer for me to go than for you, and that way he will get the message."

When he hefted the strap of the satchel over his shoulder, he instructed her to lock the door behind him, and then he risked one last glance at her. A tear slipped down her cheek.

"You don't know how much this means to me, Nico. There are so many others relying on this message. Thank you."

Everything he wanted to say clogged his tightening throat. He reached out to tuck away the stray lock tumbling free from her messy chignon and caught himself at the last moment.

But her eyes widened all the same at his failed gesture, and he dropped his hand as if burned.

"Goodbye, Sophia."

Before she could answer, he firmly shut the door behind him and hurried down the rickety stairs. Outside, the wind blew as harsh as ever, seeping up the sleeves of his cloak. As he strolled along the street with his posters, he heard an engine rumble to life. A sleek car with a full-throated purr—not a rattling, gasping truck reserved for a farmer lucky enough to receive gasoline rations.

He forced himself to walk with purpose, neither too slow nor too fast. He had every reason to be out.

Yet the car followed him, not bothering to pass him on the cobblestone street.

His skin prickled as he casually adjusted his bag where the posters poked through. Never had he been so glad for the cover of propaganda, even as the engine idled behind him, threatening discovery and arrest. Very well. He would play their game and lead them on a wild-goose chase.

Come and follow me. That's exactly what I need you to do. Follow me and not Sophia.

The car obeyed, keeping an even pace.

But Nico refused to look. Betraying his awareness of them would make them detain him, and they weren't nearly far enough away from Sophia yet. If she stepped outside now, they would spot her in their rearview mirror and surely question her for spending the night somewhere she did not live. He could not let that happen.

So he lifted his chin and continued to place one foot in front of the other, even as the gaze of those inside the car sent prickling chills up and down his spine.

CHAPTER EIGHT

*A*fter Debbie arrived home later that night, she called Greg. "I'm sorry I missed your text earlier. Things were crazy at the café. How are you?"

"Better now," he told her, his voice warm. "Are you free tonight? We thought it would be nice to get the scent of pine in the house before the holidays."

The idea of cutting down a Christmas tree brought a smile to her lips. "I'll grab my scarf and gloves."

During the wait, she refreshed her makeup and hair, feeling a sense of anticipation as she always did when she was about to see Greg. Last year, Greg had invited her to cut down a tree with his sons. She loved the tradition of picking out a lovely tree and taking it home in the truck. Somehow, sitting beside Greg with the boys in the back felt so right. She had grown to care deeply for this family.

A pair of headlights swung into her driveway, so she slung her purse strap over her shoulder and headed outside into the crisp air.

Ever the gentleman, Greg got out of his truck and opened the door for her. She slid in, smiling from ear to ear. Jaxon and Julian greeted her from the back seat.

"Thanks for including me," she said as she buckled her seat belt. "There's nothing better than the scent of pine."

Greg chuckled as he pulled out of the driveway. "I'm often late to put up Christmas decorations. And Jaxon and Julian aren't too keen on stringing popcorn by themselves."

"It's true," Julian chimed in. "I always poke my finger on the needle, but Dad just has to have an old-school Christmas."

"Maybe we could bake gingerbread ornaments," Debbie said as she turned to look at the two teenagers. Then she dropped her voice to a whisper. "And we could eat them too."

Julian's face broke out into a toothy grin. "Now that's my kind of decorating."

Greg shot Debbie a pleased look. "That sounds wonderful. Truly wonderful."

"I've always loved the classic Christmas traditions," she admitted.

"And it's fun to start new ones too," Greg said as he braked for a stop sign. "So, I heard the social media star might be packing up to leave town."

Debbie groaned and leaned back in her seat. "It wouldn't surprise me. He wants Ricky's painting, but Ricky won't part with it, not that I blame him. In misplaced retaliation, Maurice seems to be following through on his threat to cancel the show he was going to do on the station."

"He sounds pretty determined to get what he wants," Greg said. "How are you doing with it?"

"I'm leaving the situation in Kim's hands," she replied, sounding calmer to her own ears than she felt. "It was her idea to contact *Days of Yesteryear*, and if anyone can smooth his ruffled feathers, it'll be Kim."

"That's an excellent plan," Greg agreed. "Do you need any extras for the Nativity play? What do you think, boys? Should we be shepherds or something?"

"As long as I don't have a speaking part," Jaxon said. He adjusted his knit cap, black with a white stripe, on his head. His hair had grown long over recent months. Would he cut it or continue to grow it out? What would it be like to raise teenagers? She hadn't the slightest clue.

"I think we could arrange for some nonspeaking appearances," she said. "Janet promises cookies for the volunteers. Since Ian isn't feeling well, we welcome any new helpers."

"I'm in," Julian announced.

"Of course you are." Greg chuckled. "You'll do almost anything for Janet's baking."

"Who wouldn't?" Julian retorted.

Everyone laughed.

When they reached the Christmas tree farm, Greg parked. Debbie exited the truck and paused to study the dark sky strewn with stars. She felt a wave of nostalgia for the Christmases of her childhood. What a precious gift to share these moments with Jaxon and Julian. Greg reached for her hand, and the warmth surged through her chest, bringing tears to her eyes.

"Are you okay?"

She sniffled. "I couldn't be happier. Truly. Thank you for inviting me."

He squeezed her gloved hand, his grip firm and secure. Their gazes met. Was it her imagination, or were his cheeks red? Maybe it was the cold.

They all headed toward the trees, their boots crunching on the packed snow covering the parking lot. The scent of the evergreen pines and firs filled the cold air with a sweet and spicy scent. She inhaled deeply, relishing the sharp aroma.

The teen boys suddenly became as animated as kids as they discussed the pros and cons of the different trees.

"Julian always wants to pick out the worst tree," Jaxon announced, pointing to one example with drooping branches and a pile of needles at the stump.

Debbie hid a smile, unsurprised that softhearted Julian would want to rescue the saddest tree to make sure it didn't feel left out.

"We want a good one this year. Something special," Greg said.

How she longed to make this holy season beautiful for everyone. Perhaps Greg felt the same way.

She pointed out a statuesque Douglas fir. "That would be lovely in your living room."

"I like it," Greg answered, and the boys chorused agreement.

Her phone rang in her purse, distracting her attention from Greg with his saw.

"It's Kim. I better take this," Debbie told Greg as she answered the call.

Kim didn't mince words, her voice trembling with excitement. "Debbie, I did it! I convinced Maurice Devons to stay. He was in the middle of loading his van when I drove over to his bed and breakfast. We were able to come to an agreement, thank goodness. I knew I couldn't let him walk away from our arrangement. He'll do the show."

Debbie exhaled in relief. "That's amazing, Kim. How on earth did you change his mind?"

"Well, believe it or not, he does have a soft spot for small towns. When I told him how much business he would bring to the Dennison area if he stayed, he agreed. But he has conditions."

"Oh?"

"Yes, he wants exclusive filming access to the painting. He even suggested making prints to sell, any copyright owned by Ricky. But what a neat idea if Ricky agrees. Maurice has a knack for discovering a story, and he's certain the painting has some kind of past. He searched for Nico Carosi on the internet and did some digging of his own. I'll chat with Ricky. Maybe I can patch things up between him and Maurice, and we can all start fresh."

"I know Ricky wants to find out more about the history of the painting. Perhaps this news will make him reconsider. Did Maurice tell you anything about Nico Carosi?" Debbie asked.

Kim paused. "No. He wants to meet in person. But he's excited, Debbie. Really excited. And he plans to have his crew shoot the Nativity play on the train and feature the animals. Can you imagine what kind of grant money I could land with this kind of exposure?"

Debbie could imagine, but her throat still tightened at the idea of Ricky caught in the middle. Herself too, for that matter. Yet the idea of finding out more about Nico was all too tempting. "That's wonderful, Kim. Let me know if you need help coordinating that meetup, okay?"

"Will do. Thanks, Debbie."

Debbie ended the call and slid her phone into her purse.

Greg joined her. "Ready to cut down a tree?" He leaned in, causing his woodsy cologne to waft her way.

She couldn't resist smiling at him. "You bet."

"No more phone calls," he teased, nudging her with an elbow. "We must have your undivided attention. This is serious work."

She offered him an apologetic look. "Sorry about that. Kim wanted to tell me that Maurice Devons changed his mind and wants to film the feature after all."

Greg's grip tightened on her hand. Not much, but enough for her to sense his unease. "Does he now? Well, he better behave for the ladies of the Whistle Stop Café. No more flaking out when things don't go his way."

She liked the protective side of Greg, who always had her best interests in mind. It made her feel safe and cherished. Squeezing his hand back, she said, "Perhaps it will all work out for the best. I understand Maurice found something pertaining to Ricky's painting. I think it will be worth hearing what our star has to say."

And when she got a free moment, she would do some internet digging herself. But for now, she had a family in front of her—one that wanted to include her, and she wasn't about to miss that opportunity, even for an investigation.

When Greg loaded the tree into the truck with the boys, she noticed a paper bag on the driver's seat. Inside it lay a glossy sprig of mistletoe with tiny red berries. Greg glanced at her as he slammed the tailgate shut and grinned.

She caught her bottom lip between her teeth, her cheeks surely flushed.

This would prove to be a Christmas worth remembering.

It was late that night when Debbie finally unlocked her front door and kicked off her winter boots and removed her coat.

She replayed the evening. How perfect to pop popcorn and string it on the pine branches. The boys laughed and joked as they hovered near the stove to check on the progress of the gingerbread slowly browning along the edges. The scent of spice and ginger filled the house while Christmas music filtered through a radio. She might not have reached Janet's level of baking, but she could make cookies. Everyone seemed to appreciate her effort, given how few remained uneaten on the cookie sheet.

When she stepped out of the kitchen to grab the empty popcorn bowl and bring it back to make more, she nearly bumped into Greg at the base of a ladder. He must have pulled it from the garage while she trimmed the tree. Above them, the sprig of mistletoe hung from the ceiling. It spun slowly, the berries bright. Before she realized what was happening, Greg captured her face between his palms and kissed her soundly on the lips.

"I think this should be our new Christmas tradition," he whispered into her ear.

"Debbie, I think the cookies are burning," Jaxon called from the kitchen. "I'm pulling them out now."

She beamed at Greg, then went to the kitchen.

As she helped Julian with the gingerbread cookies, it hit her that the radio was playing "Winter Weather." And the line about "collecting the kisses due me" couldn't have been more timely. It had been a wonderful evening, full of beautiful memories that would last her a lifetime.

As she sank down on her living room couch, she tried to clear her thoughts as she opened her laptop to search for information about Nico Carosi.

She found nothing. Plenty of other artists and architects were credited for a new style of art with echoes of Ancient Rome meeting art deco. It was as if Nico had never existed. She uploaded a photo of his painting to run a reverse image search.

Plenty of other Nativity paintings came up with no sign of Nico's or anything that matched it. But she would not give up just yet. Ricky's family deserved to know what had happened all those years ago. She was about to add the Carosi name to see if something might come up when she heard her phone ring from the coffee table.

Retrieving the phone, she saw Ricky Carosi's number glowing on the screen. She answered, cradling the phone between her cheek and shoulder as she deposited her laptop on the coffee table.

"Hi, Debbie. I hope you don't mind me calling so late. You know how the restaurant business is. Is this a good time to chat?"

"Certainly," she murmured.

"I'm coming over to the café tomorrow to repair the frame. Kim called me and said she's chatted with Maurice Devons. She wants me to play nice with him and talk further. She also mentioned that he might be able to help me track down my great-uncle. Do you think that's a good idea?"

Debbie shifted the phone to a more comfortable position. "I'd like to see what he's come up with. Maurice does seem to have a knack for dredging up extremely valuable antiques on his show, pieces most people wouldn't give a second glance. What if you set firm boundaries with him and see what happens? The painting is safe at the café. Between Janet and me and our customers, we've got eyes on it most of the time. I highly doubt any harm will come to it."

The line remained silent for so long Debbie began to wonder if the call had dropped. Finally Ricky said, "Okay. I'll let him examine and film it. What if its airing on national TV does drum up some answers?"

She liked the glimmer of enthusiasm in Ricky's voice.

"Now you're talking. Maurice comes across as intense and maybe a little pushy, but I think we can handle him. The business would be so good for all of us. What if we convince him to get your restaurant in on the action?"

"Have the film crew come for supper one evening at the restaurant, you mean?" Ricky mused. "I'll serve my famous Italian Christmas ice cream cake made of cannoli-flavored ice cream, tiramisu, and dried fruits."

Debbie laughed. "Between you and Janet, at this rate I'm going to need to take up running in the spring. But I like the sound of ice cream cake and tiramisu. It'll be a nice contrast with all the shortbread, sugar cookies, and fruitcake. And perhaps you could include your cousin Leo in the dinner. I'm hoping we can learn more from him."

The excitement evaporated from Ricky's tone. "Believe me, you don't want to get my cousin involved."

She wanted to ask Ricky about his attitude toward his cousin, but she didn't want to pry into her friend's personal life. If Ricky wanted her to know what was going on, he would tell her. "I've thought of something that might help me research Nico. Does your family have anything historical from that era, such as photos? If you have any of Nico himself, that would probably be helpful."

"I'll see what I can find in my grandfather's photo albums. Thank you, Debbie, for being so understanding and helpful. I truly appreciate it."

After she hung up the phone, her smile died as she pictured Maurice with his over-the-top personality. Had she overpromised when she'd claimed to be able to keep such a grandiose man in check?

And why was Ricky so averse to reconnecting with his cousin at Christmas?

She scowled at her laptop. She had a feeling that before this thing was over, she'd have even more questions, and there was no guarantee she'd get any answers.

CHAPTER NINE

Rome, Italy
December 2, 1943

Nico forced himself to keep an even pace as he headed closer to the police station and Captain Accardo.

The car that stalked him slowed when Nico marched up the sweeping steps and through the door to the station. He exhaled as the door closed behind him, cutting off the sounds of the street. He allowed himself to glance over his shoulder for the first time. The black car crawled forward, the driver peering intently to catch sight of him.

With a shudder, he straightened and found the clerk at a polished desk. "I've brought posters for Captain Accardo."

"He cannot be disturbed," the young clerk said dismissively as he reached for a fountain pen.

"I spoke with him yesterday. I understood he needed the art immediately. Will you please deliver them? I'd hate for either of us to bear the cost of not following the captain's orders."

The clerk paled.

Nico pulled several tubes from his satchel and handed them over. *"Once he approves of the design, they must go to the printers."*

"I will deliver them myself." The clerk rose from his chair.

When the man scurried away to find his superior, Nico exited the building and faded into the colorless crowd milling about the streets. Thankfully, he saw no sign of the driver who had tracked him earlier. The satchel slung over his shoulder felt extra heavy as he moved through the familiar streets.

He knew Rome, and that proved an advantage as he ducked down alleys, ensuring that no one followed him. All the while, he wondered about Sophia. Had Matteo returned to dig through the apartment? Had she taken Nico's advice to hide with his neighbor?

Nico's stomach sank when he stepped out of an alley and spied another sleek black car, nearly identical to the one that had followed him earlier. Flipping up the collar of his coat to obscure his features, he debated heading in the opposite direction.

He could no longer hitch a ride with the farmer at the old Forum, but he still needed an inconspicuous ride out of the city. As he crossed onto the sidewalk, the car slowed.

His instincts urged him to run, but he forced himself to walk as if he had nothing to hide.

Everywhere he looked, he saw German influence. Indeed, rumor had it that the German army had nearly reached Naples, intent on infiltrating all of Italy for the benefit of Mussolini. Or was it Hitler? And no doubt the Nazis were exerting every bit of influence on the Roman police force to do much more.

Could the Allies push through the southern Winter Line?

He kept his chin level as he passed a group of SS soldiers in dull gray uniforms, chatting in German outside a bistrot. It was a common occurrence since Hitler had declared Italy to be an occupied country.

Never show your fear, Nico reminded himself. All he needed was to reach the main train station. The Roma Termini's once-elegant pillars and romantic curves had been flattened into a monstrosity of brutalist architecture, thanks to Mussolini's dreams of a modern Italy. But he could hide in that station and catch a train.

His feet ached in his shoes, and the wind nipped at his cheeks as he caught sight of the immense central station. Architect Angiolo Mazzoni had completed two wings thus far, with further construction planned in the new year. The front entrance, to be lined with stout pillars with rigid symmetry, hadn't been completed yet. Once, he would have loved to have been invited to consult on such a project. Now, the imposing station that had stripped away Italy's heritage made him feel ill.

Nico found a cluster of men talking animatedly. He joined them as they pushed through the entrance doors to the grand station. White marble gleamed everywhere, cold and glossy. Arches loomed over the immense crowd of passengers, echoing the ancient world. Mussolini had intended the station to impress Hitler and intimidate everyone else.

A peek over his shoulder revealed no sign of the black car through the massive windows.

Nico bought a ticket and crowded onto the train with countless other faces in weary lines. As he took his seat, he couldn't help but note that to his left, another group of soldiers sat, their gray uniforms indicating their origin as they quietly jested in German.

The man across from him, wearing a plain suit, unfolded a newspaper, his gaze falling on Nico's satchel.

Someone shouted on the platform, and a police whistle blew shrilly.

"Trouble outside," the stranger murmured as he stared out the window.

"There's always trouble," Nico replied.

"True enough." The older man, who appeared to be in his fifties, slanted a sidelong glance at the soldiers. One had risen from his seat to see what the commotion was about. "What's in the bag?"

"Art." Nico's answer came out as a grunt.

The train jolted forward with a long hiss, followed by the shriek of a departing whistle.

The flap of the satchel slid, revealing one of the garish posters. Meanwhile, the SS soldier sank back into his seat. He must have glimpsed the artwork, for he addressed Nico. "Wofür ist das?" Nico knew some German phrases, but he stared stupidly at the blond soldier who repeated his question, pointing again to the satchel beside Nico.

"I think he's curious about your bag as well," the stranger said in a low tone. He snapped open his newspaper and hid behind it once more.

Nico pulled out the ugliest red-and-black poster with the Roman fasces, a bundle of sticks with a protruding axe the ancient Roman officials had carried during tribunal parades for the emperors.

The soldier glanced at the paper, his eyes brightening as if he'd been granted a secret handshake.

"I am an artist," Nico explained. *Meanwhile, his pulse raced like the train picking up speed. He wasn't sure if the man understood him.*

"Kannst du mich zeichnen?"

Bewildered, Nico racked his brain to make sense of it until the soldier jabbed a thumb at his chest and then gestured with his fingers against his other palm as if he might be sketching.

"Ah, you want me to draw you?" Nico found his voice even though his mouth had dried. A spark of terror ran through his veins.

"Ja!" the soldier exclaimed. "Per favore."

Please—in Nico's own tongue.

Sucking in a breath through his teeth, Nico pulled out a scrap of fresh paper and a pencil. He knew the risk of refusing such a request, and it wasn't as if he had anything else to do on the train ride. Perhaps humoring the soldier would earn him some favor. He studied the young, eager man sitting in front of him, who bore the ribbing of his three companions. They seemed to be egging him on to pose nicely. A man who would likely go on to the northern lines to do who knew what.

The sketch was loose, hurried, and without emotion. Yet as Nico handed it over, the soldier beamed widely, his teeth flashing in appreciation. "Danke."

As he replaced his pencil in the satchel, Nico noted that the man sitting across from him did not lower the newspaper or make conversation again.

He should be used to this type of reaction from those who hated what Italy had become, but it still burned him. You work for them, Sophia had said at his flat. The implications of making art to express the ideals of the Fascist party would haunt him forever.

Just how would her brother receive him when he stumbled into their camp? Would he be met with further hatred or worse? He certainly deserved whatever kind of reaction he got.

Perhaps he was a fool to try to earn redemption at long last.

He pressed a trembling finger against his lips as the train hurtled out of Rome, leaving behind all he knew and loved in favor of the dreaded barrier lines manned by Hitler's men. Some might have pined for St. Peter's Basilica, the Vatican palace, the Castel Sant'Angelo, or the Colosseum. Perhaps even the ancient Forum or the decrepit temple of the Vestal Virgins. But it was the image of the Giudice bakery, and the leather shop below his flat with its foul yet familiar stench, and his sweet old neighbor puttering about her apartment that filled his mind as the train barreled toward its destination.

Beside him, the outline of the painting beneath the leather bag brought a moment of rare comfort.

He rested his hand on the satchel and thought of the woman he had left behind. And he thought of the journey that lay ahead.

Please, Sophia, be safe.

At the village of Brisighella, Nico got off the train after a numbing ride. No one spoke to him as he gathered the posters and the Nativity painting. He stepped onto the platform, relieved to leave the soldiers.

He flipped up the collar of his coat, the weather even cooler than in Rome. Snow fell, scattering a light dusting on the dirt roads and on the tops of the buildings. He saw no inn or other place to spend the night sheltered from the unusual winter weather.

Fear took hold of him. He had money, but the villagers didn't take to strangers. One woman slammed the door in his face when he begged for a place to stay the night or a bite to eat. Perhaps, as Sophia had hinted, more of the countrymen supported the resistenza than those within the fine cities.

They likely suspected that he was an informer.

God, I need a miracle—if You are willing, *he prayed. He hadn't prayed in a very long while. For so long, he had tried to stay safe. Now it seemed danger surrounded him at every corner. As he trudged down a long road into the country, he despaired of finding lodging.*

He despaired of finding any kindness remaining in Italy.

Not that you deserve it, the fierce voice in his head scolded, and he couldn't argue with it.

Night fell, spreading a blanket of stars so vivid that they took his breath away. Framed by the light from a full silver moon, he stopped in the middle of the road. His breath fogged into the air as the chill descended through him. Glittering white covered the sloping hills leading to the mountains, while cypress trees stood straight and tall along both sides of the road. Could he find Sophia's brother on such a night?

His energy sapped, he doubted he could go much farther.

And then, in the darkness, a light flared a quarter of a mile to the north of him. A single light, but as he strained to see it, he made out the outline of a small house with a ramshackle shed attached to it. Something bleated in the distance.

He hurried to reach the little farm, trying to ignore the blisters on his feet. When he reached the door with peeling red paint, he paused with his fist poised to knock. He feared rejection yet again.

After an indecisive moment, he lowered his arm and slipped around the house and into the stable. In the gloom with the moonlight filtering through gaps in the shuttered window, he noticed a bony cow and her calf. The lean-to reeked of animals, but he discovered a pile of straw in the corner, more than enough to cushion him. As he sank onto the straw, a black shape hissed its outrage at being disturbed at such an hour.

He stretched out, murmuring to the cat, and to his surprise, it stayed. Eventually, it curled up beside his head, lending a bit of warmth.

Nico allowed his eyes to drift closed. He would take whatever happened tomorrow.

CHAPTER TEN

*D*ebbie had just filled the coffee maker on Monday morning when the door to the café opened. Outside, a bleak sky promised more snow while a snowplow scraped the last of the parking lot. The painting, its frame newly tightened by Ricky, hung on the wall for everyone to see.

Maurice strode into the café, sans his cowboy hat. He wore all black, including a new set of cowboy boots. "Debbie, Debbie, Debbie," he said smoothly as he headed her way, ignoring the rest of the crew who brought in their cases of camera and lighting equipment. "How are you this fine morning?"

She wasn't as charmed by him this time, truth be told. The first glitter of stardom had worn rather thin after his diva-like behavior. Regardless, she chose to be polite. "It is a fine morning. You and your crew have perfect timing. Janet baked extra goodies, and the coffee will be ready shortly."

"Coffee sounds wonderful," he said with a small smile. Then he leaned over the counter, lowering his voice to a confidential tone. "I fear I must apologize for my behavior the other day. I was frustrated with your friend, but I should have handled it better."

Normally, Debbie might have simply swept it aside, but she wanted to make sure Maurice understood the impact of his behavior. "Honestly, it took the wind out of our sails. We've been looking forward to this special for a while now. Your show will help bring income to our small town, and that's a big deal. It's not every day we land in front of two million viewers who might wander our way. I hope, in the spirit of Christmas, we can all come to an agreement regarding the painting."

Maurice kept close to the counter—close enough that she felt it was necessary to step back. Perhaps he noticed her discomfort, because he pushed away from the glass. "I spoke with Ricky Carosi, and I'm pleased to say that we did come to an amicable agreement to at least film the painting. I don't want to interfere with your customers, but I've got to keep the café clear to get those shots without too much interference. If you give me an hour or so, I can manage it."

She ran her sweaty palms down the sides of her jeans. "Great."

She returned to the kitchen to help Janet frost the cinnamon buns.

"So all is well with Maurice?" Janet asked as she drizzled thick cream cheese icing over a batch still warm from the oven.

"Um, I think so." Debbie hesitated, earning a suspicious glance from Janet, but to her relief, her friend didn't push her.

The morning sped past, full of omelets and cinnamon buns and plenty of sprinkled doughnuts. The café saw a steady stream of customers, many of them saying they'd heard through the grapevine that Maurice Devons was staying and filming after all. Women came in droves, giggling while picking up cookies or other treats to go. They scanned the café, eyes obviously peeled for any sign of the star.

Business was so good that Debbie couldn't see an empty table anywhere. It was almost overwhelming, but the steady sound of the cash register dinging sounded cheerful against the background of Christmas music playing over the loudspeakers.

Paulette blew out a long breath as she balanced trays in her capable hands. Her salt-and-pepper hair was held back with glittering green clips to match her striped apron. "Goodness, Debbie, you and I will have to soak our feet tonight."

"No kidding," Debbie said as she snatched a full coffeepot to refill cups. "I've been waiting for a breather, but I don't think we'll see one today."

Paulette dropped off a load of dirty plates in the kitchen. When she reemerged, she said, "I heard you got a tree with Greg."

Debbie grinned at the memory. "I did, and we had a blast. I think the boys even enjoyed stringing popcorn, and they definitely loved the gingerbread cookies."

Paulette beamed. "Those grandsons of mine have the biggest, sweetest hearts."

"Because they have the best of dads," Debbie agreed.

Paulette squeezed her shoulder then got back to work.

Debbie continued to refill coffee, but her mind was taken over by the mental image of Greg buying mistletoe. Her cheeks heated again at the thought.

She hadn't felt this excited over the holidays in years—even though she hadn't decided what to buy him yet. And what could she purchase for Jaxon and Julian that would be meaningful and treasured? Perhaps she could ask Paulette for advice when they had a moment. She was always so warm and welcoming, even encouraging Debbie to not give up on the possibility of a relationship with Greg when other women had made it clear that they were interested in him. Greg was always polite, but never reciprocated in such encounters, and Paulette had been certain it was because he only had eyes for Debbie. It turned out that she'd been right.

Debbie was pulled from her reverie when, to her delight, a familiar white-haired woman entered the café with her daughter. Eileen Palmer, wearing a vintage plum-color wool cloak with a rhinestone pin sparkling in the winter light, lit up when she saw Debbie.

"Eileen, I'm so thrilled to see you," Debbie said in greeting. "What can I get you today?"

Eileen's eyes twinkled as she touched her white curls. "I'm hoping I'll find some doughnuts remaining. Kim told me there's been a run on the café."

"Oh, yes. It's been crazy, but so much fun." Debbie winked at Kim, who was also dressed in a 1940s style. The museum director often dressed for the era when giving special presentations. Her green suit and black kitten heels were nothing short of glamorous.

"Someone dressed up today," Debbie said, adding, "You've got the best vintage fashion sense, Kim."

"Where do you think I learned it?" Kim helped her mother to the nearest free table. "I've got an interview with Maurice later this afternoon, and I wanted to look the part. Mom helped me pick the outfit." Kim appraised Debbie. "And you, my friend, certainly exude Christmas cheer."

Debbie wore red jeans with a matching sweater. Her apron, striped green and white, made her feel like an elf, but Janet had insisted on the matching outfits. Paulette had joined in the fun with a similar ensemble.

Kim ordered mochas and doughnuts, and when Debbie returned with the tray, she found Eileen staring at the Carosi painting.

"I remember that piece," Eileen said as she moved to get out of the chair.

Debbie put down the tray and offered her arm. With slow steps, the older woman approached the wall of art.

"Rafe adored that painting. He encouraged Alberto to keep it on the wall year-round. He used to say that we should feel the joy of Christmas long after the last gift had been opened."

"Sounds like wonderful advice," Debbie said.

Eileen's eyes watered. "I miss Rafe. Alberto too. They always made me feel like life was so much fun and worth celebrating. They made sure family always came first." She dashed away a stray tear. "Forgive me. I didn't expect to cry, but there is something so moving about seeing a picture of our Savior and the light falling on Him from the star above. So much hope in the humblest of settings. Rafe and Alberto would be delighted to see it enjoyed by so many people."

"Perhaps over two million, Eileen. *Days of Yesteryear* has quite the fan base, and everyone will be blessed by it."

"Isn't that something? This little oil painting remained hidden from the world for decades, tucked away in one family's home. Now so many more will enjoy it."

Debbie caught a glimpse of a man in black striding through the parking lot. Maurice Devons. "Maurice is outside now. Do you want to meet him?"

Eileen perked up, patting her hair again. "Do you think he has time in his busy schedule to chat with me?"

"It can't hurt to ask."

Maurice proved he knew how to be a gentleman when he wanted to, even bending over Eileen's hand like a rakish Clark Gable. He also signed an autograph on a travel brochure of Ohio while Debbie and Kim each snapped a photo of the two of them together.

They had barely finished when a group of *Days of Yesteryear* staff came into the café, their cheeks red from the cold.

Kim smiled at Maurice. "Mr. Devons, after I return my mother to Good Shepherd, I would be happy to lead a tour of the stationary cars. Perhaps you would like a tour of our special Christmas train too? Our interim engineer would be happy to give your staff a ride. I think it would present a charming backdrop for a video, don't you?"

No one sold the museum quite like Kim.

"I love your idea," Maurice said, "And by the way, your mother is a grand lady. I'm delighted to have made her acquaintance."

Eileen dabbed at her lips with her napkin. "Such lovely flattery, but it's rather nice to be called a grand lady. Truthfully, the station is what's grand. So many stories to tell within these walls. You could spend a month here and not discover it all."

Debbie had to agree. This past year, she and Janet had dug into several mysteries, each one more fascinating than the last. She caught Maurice's intense gaze as he studied her rather than Eileen.

His eye contact didn't waver as he said, almost wistfully, "I would very much like to see more of Dennison, but for now, I'll have to content myself with the Whistle Stop Café and the museum's wonderful hospitality. It'll be a Christmas to remember."

"Have you no family at Christmas?" Eileen asked as she patted his arm.

He shook his head, his lips pressed tightly.

Debbie felt a surge of sympathy for him. For all his fame and bravado, he appeared quite sad.

Maurice backed away from the table. "You ladies are too kind. If you don't mind, I must excuse myself and check on my staff."

As Debbie poured steaming dark roast coffee, she watched him from the corner of her eye.

He started toward the crew at the counter ordering extra coffee and goodies, but he halted at the Nativity painting on the wall. Folding his arms over his chest, he stared at it, seemingly unaware that he was blocking other guests' access to the painting or through the space to the tables.

Jude, the lead camera technician and assistant, called to his boss, "Cappuccino, Maurice?" He held up a red to-go cup heaping with foam and a dusting of cinnamon.

Debbie brought the now-empty coffeepot to the coffee maker.

Thankfully, Paulette had already started another pot. The older woman rang up orders at the register. "Debbie, can you put three spiced doughnuts in a bag for this gentleman, please?"

"Of course. You're saving us today," Debbie told her as she grabbed the tongs and pulled open the back of the display case. She snatched the last three green-frosted doughnuts and slid them into a paper bag.

Jude smiled, but it didn't quite touch his eyes as he took the bag from Debbie. He grabbed the cappuccino in one hand and the doughnuts in the other. "Hey, Maurice. Your cappuccino is ready."

Maurice removed his fist from under his chin, unfolding his long arms. He shot a glare at the young cameraman. "I want extra foam. And no cinnamon."

"Well, la-di-da," the cameraman muttered. He grimaced apologetically to Paulette. "Can you remake this, please? Extra foam and no Christmas cheer for Mr. Grinch over there."

Paulette's eyes went as round as saucers. "I'm so sorry. We've never had a complaint about the foam before."

Jude's upper lip curled. "It's not you. It's him. Welcome to a mere taste of my world."

Debbie placed a hand on Paulette's shoulder. "I'll get the cappuccino." She made it as quickly as she could with extra foam and brought it to Maurice.

"Extra foam. No cinnamon." She kept her response measured since Maurice's high-handed treatment would obviously continue.

He took the cup, his hand brushing against hers—the gesture seemingly absentminded since he kept his attention on the painting. "Have you noticed the wear and tear on this artwork?"

"I'm not really an art expert," Debbie said, but she stepped closer to the painting all the same.

Jude came to stand beside her. His hand hovered over the painting, but he didn't touch it. Instead, he tucked his hand back into his coat pocket. "There's wear between the seams of the frame, and it was loose the other day. Should it be on the wall? I bet it could easily be restored."

She shook her head. "Ricky fixed it. As long as no one touches the canvas, it should be fine."

Maurice harrumphed before pinning her with a look. "All antique paintings show some signs of age, but this one?" His finger hovered over the brushstrokes of the manger and then traced a nearly invisible path to the frame. "This one shows so much damage."

Debbie forgot her ire with the man and leaned forward. Once her eyes adjusted to the exquisite detail, the lifelike realism of Mary and Jesus, she noted several scratches etched into the canvas.

The wood, too, appeared almost rugged where the canvas met the frame. She gasped when she saw a row of tiny holes marring the entire frame and the edge of the canvas. "What are these? Why haven't I noticed them before?"

Maurice sent her an approving glance. "The sunlight is coming in brighter today, and it's hitting the painting at the right angle. Can you see the pencil marks leading to the star? Now, that is unusual. Why would the artist put pencil marks over the oil?"

She peered closer. Indeed, a soft mark etched a path to the Bethlehem star.

"And it's as if the canvas has been stretched over and over again. That explains the holes, but I wonder why it was restretched so many times." He shook his head. "If I could get an art restorer to rub the painting, we could test and discover what kind of paints comprise this. Restorers do it on a regular basis, cleaning, and relining if needed, and—"

"No," Debbie answered firmly. "You can film the piece, but that's the extent of it, per your agreement with the owner. However, I confess, I want to know more about the artist, Nico Carosi. Did you find anything? I've run into a dead end with my search online."

Maurice ran a finger across his pinched lips. Would he respect her refusal, or would he push further? And would he use her denial as a reason not to help?

He finally spoke. "I believe it may have been painted during the Fascist reign of Mussolini, who called for a second future of art. He intended for the buildings and murals to act as propaganda. Not every artist survived the regime, and those who did often painted exclusively for Mussolini. They didn't exactly want to broadcast their work after the war ended."

"Ricky Carosi told me that his great-uncle went missing after the war."

"Interesting." Maurice raised his hand and flicked a finger at his staff, the movement signaling the return of the imperious star. "It's getting late. Come on, Jude. Let's take a look at the Christmas train for filming the play that Kim talks about so much." Maurice glanced down at Debbie. "Are you playing a role?"

"An angel," she answered.

"Perfect," he said as he brushed past her, leaving a trail of overpowering musk. Maurice glared at Victor and Jude. "Honestly, guys, you can't be coming in here for pastries like this. We're not on endless coffee breaks." He tapped his watch while glaring at his staff. "Chop, chop. Let's get back to work."

Kim helped Eileen rise from the table. The museum director slanted a worried frown at Maurice, whose chiding grew louder. "I'm going to take Mom home and come right back to the station. Right back."

"I'll hold down the fort," Debbie answered. She eyed the irate celebrity. *I hope.*

CHAPTER ELEVEN

Outside of Brisighella, Italy
December 3, 1943

The sound of a cat purring next to Nico's neck woke him. Morning light streamed in to where he lay on the straw. He struggled to regain his bearings until the escape from Rome flooded back to him. He shifted ever so slightly, and the cat mewed in protest, snuggling closer with one paw on Nico's chest.

It blinked great green eyes and yawned when Nico inched away, finally wiggling free while his thoughts returned to his cramped flat and Sophia. Had she evaded Matteo? The more he thought about it, the more Nico doubted she could return home. Matteo would catch her eventually and drown her in false charges. Should Nico have taken her with him? Things had escalated so quickly, and he feared his hasty decision might prove disastrous in the end. Fists clenched, he tried to calm down and failed.

The cow and calf also watched him as the faint light of dawn crept through the gaps in the shutter of one small window.

He ached everywhere, but at least he was warm enough. He needed a miracle—several, in fact—but so far, he remained alive and well. Was his stay in this meager stable nothing more than blind luck, or had God heard his prayer the previous night?

He prayed again. Please give Sophia a miracle too.

Suddenly, the door to the stable opened, and a tiny woman shuffled inside with a bucket of feed. Her white hair was covered with a faded red scarf, and a matching shawl was tied around her hunched shoulders. She halted at the sight of him, the bucket slipping from her shaking grasp.

"Francesco? Is that you?" The hope in her eyes was bright as she gazed at him in the shadows.

"I'm sorry. I am not Francesco." Nico raised both hands, fully aware of the disheveled sight he must present. He needed a shave, and his clothes carried bits of straw and dust. "Please," he said in a low voice. "I won't hurt you. I just needed shelter for the night. I will leave immediately."

He slowly moved toward her and righted the spilled bucket, and then scooped the scattered feed back into it. "I won't hurt you. Please don't be afraid."

She sighed. "You resemble my grandson. He was to return home this week."

A soldier perhaps? Or a member of the resistenza?

Nico stood and picked up the bucket. "May I help you with chores to thank you for your hospitality?"

She let him move past her to pour the feed into the trough. When the cow and the calf finished eating, he opened the latch to their stall and led the cows into the morning light. "Do you have a well, Buona Madre? I will water your animals."

"How very kind."

But when she pointed to the well, the door to the cottage slammed and a middle-aged woman stomped outside, wiping her hands on her frayed apron. Her clothing, her shoes, and everything else about her spoke of hardship.

"Who are you and what are you doing in our home?" the younger woman demanded.

"I needed shelter last night and took advantage of your stable. I meant no harm. If you wish, I'll pay you for the night." Belatedly, he realized he had left his satchel on the pile of straw.

"He's caused no harm, Eva. He's a young man, like our Francesco. Like the others who have come our way. Let us show him hospitality," the white-haired woman said.

The younger woman, with her black hair loosely clasped in a bun, held up a warning hand. "Hush, Madre. Not another word from you."

A sliver of relief threaded through Nico as he listened to the exchange. Perhaps others with the resistenza had come this way.

The white-haired woman ignored the younger one, instead saying to Nico, "I am Catalina Aleppo, and this is my daughter, Eva. You needn't worry about working or paying us for your stay in our stable."

"It would be a dishonor to my upbringing to return such kindness with nothing."

He drew water from the stone well, the icy droplets sliding down his already chilled hands, then finished a few other chores around the stable despite Eva's grumblings. The moment she stepped out of the stable, he found his satchel and checked on the rolled posters and the painting, pausing only to retrieve the necessary coins from the depth of the bag. To his dismay, he noticed the frame of the painting had come loose. He pulled it out, studying Mary and Jesus in the dim light. The canvas was the same as always, but the gold leaf had already worn at the corners from his travels.

When the door opened, he jerked backward, but Catalina's diminutive form filled the narrow doorway—not her irate daughter. He closed the satchel flap, quickly hiding the propaganda posters, and handed the white-haired woman the coins.

"Please take them," he said in a low voice.

She studied him for a moment as if on the verge of refusing, but finally accepted the meager offering. "Where have you come from?"

"Rome," he answered truthfully. "I have a long way to go yet, if you would be so kind as to tell me—" He swallowed hard. How could he put in words his need to find the band of resistenza warriors hiding in the mountains without exposing innocent people? He didn't trust easily, a hard-learned lesson. "Can you tell me about the area beyond the mountains?"

Her eyes narrowed momentarily, taking full stock of him. Even though she had initially mistaken him for a loved one, she seemed as sharp as could be. Her gaze fell to the painting in his hand. She gasped. "Where did you find such beauty?"

"I painted it, Madre," he admitted slowly, realigning the frame so she could see Mary and Jesus better.

Her eyes watered with tears as she touched the gilded frame. Bits of gold clung to the tips of her work-worn fingers. "Our holy church lost its mural at the beginning of the war. Such a gift you have."

However, when Eva returned to the stable, she merely grunted when Catalina pointed out the Savior.

Instead, Eva glared at Nico. "You best get on your way. I don't want trouble on my doorstep, and I'll thank you to leave us be."

"I completely understand. I will go now." He bowed slightly. "Thank you for letting me stay as long as I have."

The sullen daughter slammed the door, but the old woman came close and cupped his cheek with her hand. "Don't you worry about Eva. Her heart hurts from many things. Please forgive her."

"There's nothing to forgive," Nico assured her.

She patted his cheek then pointed. "You must go northeast of the stable. In about three miles, you will find a rocky outcropping that resembles a sheep, and there I believe you will find what you are looking for."

He murmured his thanks. Was she one of the supporters that Sophia had described—a villager who brought medicine and food to those living in the hills?

Catalina smiled at last, revealing two missing teeth. "Such a sweet boy. And so alone during our holy season of Christmas. If you wish, come back and I will feed you. My table is always open for those searching for family."

When she left him, he slid the painting into the satchel among the tightly rolled posters, including the loose one the SS soldier had fawned over. Perhaps he should burn the posters—yet something held him back.

The posters had ensured his safety at the station. Perhaps if he crossed more checkpoints, they would continue to prove his alibi. Or, when he did find the resistenza, his undoing. He wasn't sure. He wasn't sure about a lot of things anymore.

As he slung the satchel over his shoulder, his heart felt fuller than he could remember. When he tried to refuse the food Catalina offered, she chided him as any nonna would do until at last, he agreed to the loaf of bread. Had she given him all she had? He hoped not.

Nor did he resent the fierce daughter, who would continue to watch out for her mother as any proper daughter would do.

The sun had begun to sink toward the horizon when he found the rock formation in the rounded shape of a sheep. Beyond it, a faint strip of smoke reached to the sky. No doubt the fire was a risk, and yet a necessity due to such a frosty winter.

He had experienced two miracles so far—safe travel out of Rome and shelter overnight.

But he needed far more divine intervention on this pilgrimage if he was to survive. By the end of the day, Lord willing, he would face Sophia's brother.

CHAPTER TWELVE

Debbie rubbed her neck as she flipped the Closed sign later that afternoon.

Janet brought bright green folders with copies of the Nativity play script to the table as the door opened.

Greg waved with Jaxon and Julian following close behind. "Your shepherds are here to report for duty," he announced as he pulled off his hat. He and the boys removed their coats, slinging them over the nearest chairs, along with an assortment of gloves and scarves.

Janet rose from her chair, motioning to the counter. "Boys, come help me bring out the bribes for our excellent cast, and you'll get first pick of the treats. Let's ruin supper for you." She went behind the counter.

"Oh man." Julian rubbed his stomach. "Any sugar cookies left?"

Greg sat beside Debbie while his sons chatted with Janet. He smelled nice—all pine and frosty winter with a hint of spice. She felt herself relax in his presence.

"You look like an adorable elf," he said in a low voice.

She glanced down at the striped apron. "Janet's idea. She gets these visions of coordinating T-shirts and aprons, and I am completely helpless to resist her machinations."

"It's pretty cute."

She beamed up at him as he wrapped an arm around her shoulders.

Julian brought a plate of cookies while Jaxon put two tables together to make more seating, as directed by Janet.

Janet sneezed into the crook of her elbow.

Debbie straightened. "Oh, not you too."

Janet waved a dismissive hand. "I'm fine. It's an allergic reaction to the pine boughs or something."

"Is Ian any better?"

"Getting there. The doctor said it's a cold and he'll simply have to ride it out," Janet answered, but Debbie didn't miss the dark shadows beneath her dear friend's eyes.

Within minutes, the other actors trickled into the café. Brad entered and then Liza, then Kim, followed by Janet's father, Steve, who joked about the weather. Harry arrived, brushing flakes from his coat. Ricky entered last, carrying a small messenger bag. The group was nearly complete except for Debbie's father.

She caught a glimpse of a figure rushing past the café window. It happened so fast she didn't see anything but a beige coat with a hood pulled over the head. Whoever it was, they would see that the café was closed and probably come back another time.

The afternoon readings proved to be a welcome balm. Jaxon and Julian played their roles as shepherds with gusto, each clearly trying to outdo the other. Their spirit quickly caught on, and soon the whole rehearsal was as lively as anyone could have wished.

It was brought to a screeching halt when Jude entered the café with a sheepish expression. "I'm sorry to interrupt, but is it too late to get some snacks to go?"

Taking pity on him after what she'd witnessed between him and his boss, Debbie ushered him to the counter and found a paper bag. "What do you need?"

"Late night food," he said, trying to stifle a yawn.

"I've got cookies left. Will that work?"

"That sounds great." He paid her and glanced over his shoulder to see what the others were doing. "Working on the Nativity play?"

"Yes, this is our rehearsal," she said, hoping he would take the hint to go.

He didn't, instead leaning against the counter while watching the group. He seemed to be in no hurry to exit the café in favor of the swirling snowflakes and bone-chilling cold outside.

Debbie returned her attention to the Nativity. When it was Kim's turn, she acted with great aplomb, as if she had been born for the stage. "And there were shepherds living out in the fields nearby, keeping watch over their flocks at night. An angel of the Lord appeared to them, and the glory of the Lord shone around them, and they were terrified." Then her phone dinged, and she read the screen. "Oh my goodness, I completely forgot. I'm supposed to lead a tour around the yard right now."

Janet waved her away. "I'll read your lines."

"Thank you. I'll catch up with you when I can." Kim hurried out of the café.

Greg got to his feet and pointed toward the ceiling, his expression alarmed. "Lo, a great angel!"

Julian chuckled as he brushed the cookie crumbs from his fingers. "Less is more when acting, Dad."

Debbie raised her hands to deliver her line. "Do not be afraid. I bring you good news that will cause great joy for all the people. Today in the town of David a Savior has been born to you. He is the Messiah, the Lord. This will be a sign to you: You will find a baby wrapped in cloths and lying in a manger."

She found her gaze sliding to the painting and then to Ricky, who also stared at it. Tonight, after the practice, she would share with him what Maurice had told her earlier about the pencil marks, as well as his claims that the canvas had been restretched several times.

Greg cleared his throat, drawing her attention back to him. He arched an eyebrow.

She was so busy trying to keep track of everything, she'd nearly missed her line. She brought her attention back and said, "Glory to God in the highest heaven, and on earth peace to those on whom His favor rests."

The door opened with a cheerful jingling of the bell. Debbie paused as a black-haired man, with a hint of gray at the temples, entered the café. A few snowflakes remained caught in his beard and mustache. He was vaguely familiar, even though Debbie hadn't met him before.

"Sorry to intrude, but I'm looking for Kim Smith. I'm Leo Carosi, the replacement train engineer."

Debbie greeted him warmly and offered her hand to shake, which Leo did vigorously, flashing a smile full of white teeth. She liked him immediately. "I'm Debbie Albright, one of the owners of the Whistle Stop Café. Kim's out back in the yard, giving a tour to some guests. Do you need help to find the place?"

He shook his head, good humor still pulling at his mouth. "No, I used to run trains here years ago. I know my way around. I'll find her. Love what you've done here, though. A café is perfect for the station."

"Thank you. We're so glad you could step in to help out. Seems like the flu is going around."

He pushed on the door. "Right you are. I do what I can to avoid getting any germs." Then Leo froze, the jovial twinkle in his eyes hardening. "Ricky."

"Leo." Ricky's flat acknowledgment came from behind Debbie. "Welcome home. It's been a while."

A gust of wind and snowflakes brushed against the café windows as Leo scowled. Debbie shivered despite the cozy heat of the café and wrapped her arms around herself. The frosty glare between the cousins was enough to freeze anyone.

Leo merely grunted in reply, but as he pivoted on his work boots, he glanced at the wall of art. "You put Grandfather's painting in the café?" The horror in his voice sharply contrasted with his previously friendly demeanor. "How dare you! Ricky, you knew how much it meant to me, and now you've displayed it in a public café without even talking to me first?"

Debbie raised her hands, stepping between the Carosi men. "It's on loan for our Christmas festivities. It will be returned to Ricky safe and sound by the end of the week. I promise you—"

"That should have been my painting. Grandfather intended it for me, not you. You got the restaurant and everything else," Leo growled, to Debbie's shock.

By now, the rehearsal had ground to a halt. Liza and Brad had stopped chatting, and even Harry appeared uncomfortable as he coughed behind a fist.

"This is not the place to discuss our private family affairs," Ricky replied steadily, but Debbie noticed he looked pale.

"We're not family," Leo snapped. He stormed out the door, nearly running into Debbie's father on his way.

"Did I miss something?" her dad asked as he removed his felt fedora.

Ricky cast an apologetic look around the group. "I'm sorry, everyone. It's a long story, and we have a play to practice. Shall we continue?"

Jude went to the door. "Thanks for the cookies. I'm heading out for the evening, but the film crew will be here bright and early. Good luck with the new train engineer. He seems an unpleasant fellow."

She frowned, wishing Jude would lower his voice.

He didn't notice. "Can't wait to see the performance on the train. Great job, everyone." He waved and ducked out the door.

The Nativity play continued, but the good humor and high energy were long gone, especially when Brad muttered to Liza, "Typical Ricky. He seems nice on the outside, but watch your back with him. He always burns his bridges."

Debbie frowned at the young man, who flushed. Ricky had always been a good friend to her, Kim, and Eileen. Of course, not everyone was equally liked in a small town, and Ricky ran a busy restaurant, hiring teenagers with frequent turnover. He was tough but fair. But she had always thought him to be kind. Why would Brad say such a harsh thing about him?

Perhaps later she could set the record straight and advise Liza to ignore Brad's gossip.

"The angel wings were delivered to my house today." Janet grinned as she waved her phone with a picture of a feathery concoction. "Ian texted me about the delivery and says hi to everyone. Debbie and I will wear white tunics with silver and gold belts. Ian can give Greg one of the shepherd costumes."

"I ordered extra shepherd costumes for Jaxon and Julian. They should be on my front steps in a day or two," Debbie added. Thankfully, almost everyone had their costumes.

"When are you bringing the animals?" Debbie asked Brad.

"Soon," he said, trying to conceal a yawn.

"I need something more concrete than that," she prodded gently. "Janet and I will arrange for safety cones to block out the area for the donkey and sheep. Otherwise, we might have every parking spot filled, thanks to Maurice Devons."

Brad shrugged one shoulder. "Never saw the appeal to *Days of Yesteryear*, but all right. I'll try to come after the café closes tomorrow. How about that?"

"Fine," Debbie agreed.

Ricky hurried out the door before Debbie could ask him any further questions about the painting. Brad sniffed as he watched Ricky leave.

"Can you close up tonight?" Janet asked Debbie. "I'm going to get more medicine for Ian. He's fighting a sore throat."

"Tell Ian to rest." Debbie waved as her friend and business partner headed with Liza out into the cold evening. Greg and his sons followed.

She sighed as she turned to finish closing the café while evening fell. At last, she put on her coat and mittens then shut off most of the lights in the café.

The back door to the kitchen rattled.

She froze, certain she was imagining things. After all, the wind brushing against an old building brought plenty of eerie sounds.

It rattled again. Very distinctly and with force.

Sucking in a breath, she flipped on the light switch. When she went to open it, she saw no one. Large footprints marred the snow, marking a path around the building. Strange. Why would someone try to access a back door? The cold wind, mingled with stinging snowflakes, chilled her face, urging her into the warmth of the kitchen. She closed the door and made certain everything was locked. Normally, she didn't worry so much about such things in a safe little town like Dennison. But tonight, it felt important.

After all, if someone had tried the back door, there was no telling what else they might try. With everything that had already gone wrong this Christmas season, Debbie was taking no chances.

CHAPTER THIRTEEN

Outside of Brisighella, Italy
December 3, 1943

Night fell earlier in the mountains, it seemed. Nico trudged through the foothills as darkness blanketed his surroundings. He despaired of finding anyone at such a late hour.

But at last, he smelled the sharp tang of smoke from a campfire on the frigid breeze. He pushed forward through the bluffs and juniper trees. There was no path, and the going was treacherous in the dark. He tripped, scraping his hands and knees against the unforgiving ground. He forced himself back up, brushing pebbles from his burning palms, and there it was—a glimmer of fire in the hollow of a cave.

He might be approaching anyone. Danger lurked everywhere. But the message, which he still had not read as he'd promised, was tucked safely inside the painting. He had come this far. He must see the task through. He began to wonder what he should do afterward. Part of him desperately wanted to return to Sophia, and part of him dreaded bringing more trouble to her.

He wished he could ask Nonna for advice, but he could only breathe a prayer as he shifted the heavy satchel higher on his aching shoulder. Though he tried to be quiet as he stumbled up the rocky hillside, his boots crunched on the ground.

"Halt! Who is that?" a man's voice demanded.

He stopped. "A friend, I hope. I seek shelter, and I saw your fire."

"No one comes here for shelter," the man replied.

A rough hand shoved Nico forward. He tried to peek over his shoulder at the shadowy figure behind him, but by now, night had swathed everything in black.

"Since you want our fire so badly, come and pay your respects," another rough voice snarled from his left.

He found himself dragged into the cave, following a sharp bend which hid most, but not all, of the fire's red glow. Inside the dank space sat about a dozen men who glared at him with such ferocity, he nearly flinched.

He gulped as someone yanked on his arm, forcing him to sit down on the stump of log dragged into the cave to form crude seating.

"Nico Carosi?" the man directly across from him asked. "What are you doing here?"

Nico scarcely recognized the man with the bushy black beard and rugged coat with missing buttons. "Hello, Paolo. I've come on behalf of your family."

"He's a spy. Don't trust him," an angry voice snapped, but Nico kept silent, forcing himself to appear relaxed.

An older man, his heavy beard threaded with white, snatched Nico's bag and dragged out the contents for all to see, including the propaganda posters. The painting followed, roughly cast onto the rock-strewn ground.

Silence ensued. Other than the hiss, pop, and crackle of flames, the men were deadly silent. All eyes were trained on Nico.

He held up both hands. "I can explain."

The voices exploded all at once. "He's with the polizia!"

Nico raised his voice to be heard over the din. "I am not with the polizia. It's true that I've painted for the party, much to my shame. Those posters allowed me to get past the checkpoints to give you a message. But I'm here on behalf of a friend in danger. And I won't say anything further until I speak with Paolo alone."

The men began to argue, their voices rising and falling as they gestured at Nico.

"What do we do with him?" someone demanded.

"Question him, of course. See what he knows. It might give us a lead on the enemy for a change."

"We are doomed!" another man cried.

For his part, Nico focused on taking even, steady breaths. He gently picked up the painting and set it on top of his leather satchel to prevent further damage. He would have to examine it later.

Sophia's brother finally raised his hand for quiet. "Enough. I will speak with Nico alone. I know him from our school days. He lived near my father's bakery." As an afterthought, he added softly, "And my sister knew him."

Paolo unfurled his tall frame, the dancing flames casting twisted shadows along the jagged rock walls. His eyes glittered as he gestured for Nico to follow outside the cave. "Come. You'd better explain yourself."

Outside the cave, the moon freed herself from the clouds, illuminating the landscape with a cold light while Nico shared the story of Sophia's near brush with the secret police and, he hoped, her escape to his neighbor's apartment.

Paolo paced back and forth in front of a stand of trees. "Ah, Sophia. What have you done now?" He pivoted to Nico, his expression difficult to read in the shadows. "What is the message then?"

Nico jammed his chilled fingers into his pant pockets, the familiar stub of the pencil waiting for him within the depths. "I didn't read it. We thought it best if I didn't know too much in case the SS soldiers caught me. It's in the frame of the Nativity painting, along with some money."

Paolo dragged a hand down his face. "She should have come with you."

"She said she had an alibi and no one saw her face. She planned to come here, but I encouraged her to stay, thinking she would be safer in Rome than traveling alone, with soldiers at every checkpoint. We can hope her contacts with the resistenza there will help her should trouble arise."

"You are ready to be a part of the resistenza?" Paolo's question pierced through the quiet night.

Alberto's warning came back to Nico. Someday you'll have to make a choice. But what will it cost you if you do nothing?

"Why did you help my sister?"

Paolo's next question came before Nico could articulate an answer to the first. He fingered the *pencil stub in his pocket again for comfort. How to answer such a question? Dare he admit what he had felt for Sophia since they were thirteen years of age? Should he say that he was tired of complying with men whose actions stained his soul? Did he confess that he desperately missed family and friends, especially at Christmas, when memories of beauty and laughter and goodness filled his mind?*

And then his answer became clear.

"It was the right thing to do," he told Paolo. "I will return to her as soon as I can. I won't see her come to harm. I promise."

Paolo blew out a noisy breath. "No one is more clever than Sophia. She has stood on her own two feet for the past three years. Why, she single-handedly—" He caught himself. "Show me the painting again."

By the time they returned to the cave, all of Nico's posters had been hauled from their cardboard tubes. One already burned in the flames, Mussolini's robust features withering into ash.

"Stop!" Paolo shouted. "I have use for those posters."

The men grumbled as Paolo shouldered his way through them. At Nico's direction, he picked up the painting and used a pocketknife to pry the canvas loose from the frame.

Nico bit the inside of his cheek when the knife nicked the edge of the canvas. It's just a painting, he reminded himself.

The men crowded around Sophia's brother. Nico realized with a small start that Paolo seemed to be the leader, at least of this pocket of the resistenza.

Paolo warned everyone to stand back as he extracted the message and the money. "I will read it in private. Not a word from any of you that would implicate our contacts to our guest. I beg each of you to remain silent."

No one spoke while Paolo read the note before flinging it into the fire to burn with the poster, now a glowing heap of ash and embers.

"Well?" one middle-aged man asked. "Do we return home?"

"We are to stay the course and finish our task here until the path clears," Paolo answered firmly.

Curious. Apparently, they were receiving orders from someone.

Paolo handed Nico the painting, its frame dangling. "Would you be willing to deliver a message to town, along with a poster to hang at the post office? As you said, you crossed the enemy lines without any trouble. Perhaps your art is exactly the cover we need."

Nico gaped at him. "What about your family?"

"I can't help them at this moment," Paolo answered regretfully. "If anything happens, it would take us days to travel to Rome, which means it would already be too late for Sophia. I cannot ride the train like you, nor can my men. Our faces are known."

"I cannot leave your sister to Matteo."

Paolo jerked as if he had been struck. "Matteo?" His voice roughened. "The chief of the secret police? The same boy we went to school with?"

"Yes. He claimed to have recognized Sophia. She delivers the bakery orders throughout the district, even to the police."

Paolo's gaze flickered. "And you said she went to your neighbor?"

"I hope she did," Nico replied firmly. "My neighbor, Mia Ginerva, is trustworthy."

"Trustworthy friends are difficult to find these days. I will pray Mia takes care of my sister. We fret over her, Nico, but she is far stronger than you realize. Far cleverer too. This is as much her fight as it is mine. It's been a reckoning long in the making. Can any of us forget when soldiers—our own people—dressed in black and marched on Bolzano in 1928?"

"We were children then," Nico said. "We didn't understand what was happening."

"Sophia did. Even though she was a young girl, she knew evil when she saw it," Paolo replied.

Nico met Paolo's gaze and cringed. When they were boys, they had been forced to wear black with other comrades and join the Opera Nazionale Balilla for the Italian youth. From ages eight to fourteen, they'd been in the balilla. In school, the teacher would demand, "To whom the victory?" He and all the others had to shout back, "To us!"

As fourteen-year-olds, they had exchanged one black uniform for another when forced to join the avanguardisti. He had gone along with all of it, too afraid to see his family arrested—or worse.

Yet while many Italians chose complacency, Paolo and Sophia had always chosen to rebel.

Paolo leaned toward Nico. "With Hitler's men invading our land and taking away our neighbors to their camps, you must understand how important our fight is. We all must sacrifice to secure our freedom."

His words rang too close to those Alberto had said to Nico.

"One trip to town," Paolo pressed. "That's all I'm asking. A driver is bringing us supplies tomorrow. He will give you a ride to the village. He's a local farmer named Francesco. You will hang a poster at the post office and give the postmaster, Salvatore Rossi, my *message to be telegraphed to Sicily. He will likely have a message waiting for you to bring to me. Afterward, you can decide what you do with your life. But if you really want to help my sister, you'll agree to this."*

CHAPTER FOURTEEN

Early on Tuesday morning, Debbie returned to work. But rather than enter through the front as she usually did, she ducked around back to the kitchen door. Enough snow had fallen during the night to blur the tracks. The harsh wind also created small drifts, obscuring details. She hadn't imagined the door rattling. Someone had tried to enter the kitchen when the café appeared deserted. Why would they choose that particular door? Had she frightened the person away when she flipped on the lights?

She shivered in the biting wind. Winter was especially brutal this year. She hurried inside.

She found Janet baking cherry tarts in the kitchen.

"Hey, someone tried to enter through the kitchen door last night when I was closing."

Janet raised an eyebrow. "That's weird."

"I also saw someone with a beige parka walking outside the café when we all gathered for the Nativity play, but I didn't think much of it. I'm sure it was nothing."

"Maybe ask Kim if it could have been the janitor," Janet suggested. "It might have been one of Maurice's TV crew. Or could it be Tim, Brad's father?"

"But I don't see why any of them would try to open our back door, especially when the lights were off in the café." Debbie made a mental note to chat with Kim as soon as she got a free moment. She'd find time between running the café and the meeting she'd arranged with Ricky the previous evening.

She had to smile as she got to work. *Never a dull moment.*

After the morning rush, Debbie sat with Ricky in the café. Paulette was working and had the few occupied tables well in hand.

Ricky pulled an envelope from his coat pocket and removed a faded sepia photo. "That's my grandfather and Nico as boys."

Debbie examined the two smiling boys in the photo, arms thrown around each other's shoulders. "They were obviously close at one time."

"It seems like it. I hope we learn something soon. That would be great timing during the holidays," Ricky said as he typed on his slim laptop.

They spent Debbie's break studying the canvas while searching again for a style similar to Nico's. Neither of them could make sense of the pencil marks pointing to the star of Bethlehem.

"What were you trying to tell us, Nico?" Debbie murmured.

"The wise men followed the star to find the Messiah," Ricky said. "Perhaps that is all Nico wanted to indicate, but I'm not sure why he did it in pencil. Unless he meant to fill it in with paint later, but never got the chance. I'm not an artist. I can't understand why he painted the way he did."

She considered his suggestion. "You think the painting might be unfinished?"

"Perhaps," Ricky admitted. "I don't see how we could know without talking to Nico himself."

"Maurice mentioned futurism as an art style. Can we narrow our search to that phrase?"

Ricky's fingers flew across the keyboard. An article popped into view. He angled the screen so she could read with him.

"I can't read Italian," she said.

He hit a button and changed the words to English.

She scanned the article on Mussolini's desire for propaganda, especially in architecture and art as Hitler had done in Germany. A Ministry of Popular Culture had been formed in 1937 with the purpose of "educating" the public and refuting any arguments against fascism.

But it was the efforts of a special unit in 1935, she read, that became the strong arm of the movement, spreading art through murals in public buildings and tearing down the older monuments and buildings. Such actions moved the country further into Mussolini's control. Handshakes, top hats, and afternoon tea were replaced with Roman salutes and militaristic marching. French, American, and English literature were labeled immoral and banned from public libraries. An art show, the Augustan Exhibition of Romanità, was organized to celebrate the anniversary of the birth of Emperor Augustus. It was a significant event, connecting the fascist regime with the perceived glory of ancient Rome.

She spotted a photo of artists in front of a library. "Could Nico have been a part of the propaganda exhibition?"

"He would have been very young, perhaps seventeen at the time," Ricky mused.

"Teenagers often want to belong. I can't imagine the peer pressure during such a time, especially if most Italians followed Mussolini, or at least found it safer not to openly resist him." Debbie peered at the grainy photo showcased in the article.

Ricky enlarged the article and pulled out his creased photo to compare the pictures.

Ricky's photo showed Alberto, his arm draped around a tall, skinny kid with a shock of black hair. In the article photo, a tall man with tousled curls stared at the photographer with a somber expression. The boyish smile was nowhere to be seen, but the face appeared to be the same, despite the years between the two pictures.

"I think that is Nico standing with the other artists," Debbie said as she studied the computer screen. "They all seem to be wearing the same black uniform too."

"The uniform of Mussolini's youth program. He required it." Ricky rubbed the back of his neck. "Debbie, I can't help but assume the worst of Nico. I have no choice but to accept that my grandfather was right all along. Nico was a traitor all those years. It wasn't simply art. It was a way of life—the worst sort of life."

She put a hand on her friend's arm. "Maybe you're right. Your grandfather saw the danger and got out of Italy before it was too late. He was such a courageous man to leave all he loved behind."

"He always loved America. He said there was nothing more important than preserving freedom and the rights of man. He emigrated with hardly anything to his name, other than his desire to work and start a fresh life." Ricky ran a finger over his grandfather's features in the old picture. "I don't know what to think now, Debbie. I feel sick about Nico and the painting."

Debbie frowned. She couldn't blame her friend for feeling sad. But should Ricky give up on Nico so soon? "Take a break from the search, Ricky, and try to enjoy Christmas with your family. And know that I'm not finished yet with your great-uncle's history. When did the painting arrive in Dennison?"

Ricky scrunched his brow. "I don't know when the package was mailed exactly, but if I remember right, my grandfather thought it was during the German invasion of Italy. The American government held on to it for a while since it came from Italy. In those days, many Italian American citizens were sent to detention camps to wait for the war to end. My grandfather was lucky enough to escape that fate, but the painting languished for a good year in various customs and government offices before it reached Dennison. At that point, my grandfather hadn't seen his brother in years."

"That's a long time—long enough for a man to change his mind about many things. Perhaps Nico saw the error of his ways."

"I'd like to think so, but I'm not so sure anymore," he said quietly.

She rose. "I have to meet with Brad's father about the animals, but after the train show, we'll dig deeper, okay?"

"Fair enough." Ricky's expression relaxed a bit. "Everyone is talking about the train ride and the play. It's going to be an event to remember. I'll come later in the afternoon for the big show. My family is pretty excited to ride the train."

"I'm excited about that too."

He packed up his computer and put on his coat. "One more thing, Debbie."

"Yes?"

"When Leo accused me of getting the painting and the restaurant and everything else from Grandfather, he didn't tell the full story. I didn't get everything. Our grandfather left Leo the investments. Maybe Grandfather handled things clumsily, gifting all the sentimental things and the house and the restaurant to me, but Leo came out well enough. Besides, he never wanted to cook. So don't say anything to Leo about our search, okay?"

"All right, but in return I'd like you to consider something for me," Debbie replied.

"What's that?"

"Do you think you should patch things up with your cousin—especially for the holidays?"

Her suggestion made Ricky's mouth pucker as if he had tasted something sour. He grabbed his computer bag and slung it over his shoulder. "No. I know you think otherwise, but in my experience, people don't just change, Debbie. Trust me."

Later that morning, Kim stopped in for a coffee.

Debbie handed over the to-go cup. "By the way, Kim, someone tried to enter through our kitchen as I was closing last night. This morning, I saw footprints by the kitchen door. I wondered if you might know who it was."

Kim wrapped her hands around the warm cup. "Maybe it was Maurice. He's into just about everything and wants as many historical stories as I can feed him. I also talked with Victor, one of the camera guys, about walking around the café after he filmed some of our antiques in the museum. I'm sure it's nothing to worry about."

Debbie nodded. That made sense.

Brad entered the café with his father, Tim, who greeted Debbie warmly. He brushed snow off his beige coat. "The donkey and the sheep will be here soon. Right now my men are delivering the hay and fencing."

"I can't wait!" Debbie exclaimed. Her eagerness was rewarded as she saw a truck and trailer pulling into the parking lot.

Tim chuckled. "The donkey's a stubborn old man, but he loves kids. Plus the sheep are always a crowd pleaser."

"Hey, I thought I heard someone try to enter the back café door after the rehearsal," Debbie said casually. "Was it you, Brad?"

He shook his head. "I had to run a few errands before I went home to Dad."

She paused to watch from the window as Tim and Brad ducked out of the café to help their hired hands set up a fence with plenty of hay bales inside. A few of the morning guests brought their mugs of coffee to stand with Debbie.

Jude entered the café, pushing his newsie cap up his forehead. "I see the animals are about to make an entrance."

"Very soon. Is everything ready for you and the team to start shooting?"

"I think so. Kim showed us the stationary cars, and we got some stellar shots. I'm excited to get one of a train leaving the station." His expression was absent as he stood beside her to watch the men outside at work.

"Dare I ask if Maurice is behaving?" she asked.

Jude sent her an amused look. "Today, he's been especially nice. Promised us holiday bonuses even. So I do believe we will have a good day after all."

"Glad to hear it," she said. "Hey, did one of your staff try to get into the café kitchen last night?"

"Not that I've heard. After I got the cookies from you, Maurice sent me back to the bed and breakfast to grab his spare charger for his laptop. His old cord stopped working." Jude checked the time. "I'd better get a move on. I don't want to test Maurice's good mood." He smiled and headed toward the counter where Paulette was working the cash register.

Debbie grinned after him. If his staff felt so positive, then maybe a little Christmas cheer had rubbed off on Maurice Devons after all.

Maybe she was being tense for no reason, looking for excuses to be worried where none existed. Sure, someone had tried to enter the kitchen last night, but it might have been completely innocent. When she peered out the window again, she saw plenty of parkas in a myriad of colors. At a glance, she could see that both Tim and Victor had beige coats.

Laughter rang out around her as the guests pointed out the nearest window. The animals had arrived. Brad was red-faced as he tried to drag the ornery donkey forward. It brayed a protest and plunked down on its hind legs. Brad scowled and yanked again on the rope, finally muscling him less than a foot across the icy pavement.

"Come on, Burro, stop being so stubborn," Brad shouted as he tugged the rope.

Debbie couldn't hide her chuckle. "They named him the Spanish word for 'donkey'?"

Janet emerged from the kitchen in time to hear her question. "Actually, Brad told me they named him that because of that meaning, and because the same word is Italian for 'butter.' They wanted to reference his escape-artist tendencies to slip away, as well as Brad's culinary passion."

Someone hooted. "That donkey will be the star of the show, eh?"

She went back to work, pleased to see the grins and hear the contagious laughter of the guests. Just a few more hours and she would don her angel costume.

That evening, Debbie and Janet admired the angel wings as they shimmied into their costumes in the café kitchen before the show. They had decided to wear the white robes over khaki pants and white shirts. Debbie added her sparkling silver sash and halo, then shrugged into the elastic loops to slide the feathered white wings onto her back. They arced out behind her, large enough that she would have to angle herself to get through any doorways. Janet wore a gold sash and halo, a nice combination with her blond bob.

They both freshened their lipstick at the mirror and added extra blush. Kim had advised them that the camera would wash them out otherwise. It had been a while since Debbie had worn so much makeup, but it would be worth it in the end.

Harry, Steve, Debbie's father, Greg, Jaxon, Julian, and Liza arrived at the café in their costumes. Greg and the boys wore dark brown robes with belted green sashes. Greg even carried a wooden staff. She wondered where he had gotten it.

Greg's eyes widened when he saw Debbie emerge from the kitchen.

Self-conscious, she touched her hair, specially curled for the event. "Is my halo crooked or something?"

"No, you are absolutely beautiful. In fact, I can't decide which I like better—the Christmas Elf or the Angel." Dimples appeared on each of his cheeks.

"She's an angel, and don't you forget it, Greg Connor!" her dad called.

"Believe me, I won't," Greg answered with a grin.

Debbie groaned, then laughed.

Paulette insisted the cast line up together for a group photo near the art wall. "Move in close, everyone."

Greg wrapped an arm around Debbie's waist, careful of her wings, and the cast clustered tightly. Debbie gave her brightest smile just as Maurice entered the café, Victor right behind him. The cameraman paused near the painting and snapped a picture of the art wall. When he caught Debbie's eye, he scowled. That poor guy needed some Christmas cheer.

"One more photo," Paulette demanded. "Jaxon, no blinking. Hey, no bunny ears either, you guys."

"Aww, that's no fun," Julian complained, and both boys laughed.

Maurice flashed Debbie a quick, unreadable look as he strode to the counter. Greg still had his arm around her waist. The host of *Days of Yesteryear* cleared his throat, drawing attention to himself.

"I'd like to get some video of you all giving your lines," he spoke to the cast. "We won't necessarily tape the entire performance, but when you move through the cars, remember to speak loud and clear.

My technicians can edit the sound, but the clearer it is to begin with, the better it'll come out. It's going to be a full train if the crowd outside is anything to go by."

"You'll be riding the train?" Debbie asked Maurice.

"I wouldn't miss it for the world."

Jude dashed into the café with his camera. "I think we're ready. I just saw the engineer climb aboard. I'll get the money shots for that Christmas bonus you promised." He winked at Maurice.

Maurice slapped Jude on the shoulder. "Good man. I can't wait to see what you come up with."

Paulette finally looked satisfied with the photos she'd taken. "Have a great time on the train, everyone. I hope someone will record the entire play and not leave it all to Maurice. I want to see that recording tonight."

"Harry's got Patricia doing the honors," Debbie assured her. "We'll have video of your grandsons. You're sure you don't mind running the till and serving cocoa and cookies?"

Paulette patted her arm. "Someone's got to do it. Most of the crowd will probably be on the train with you anyway. I doubt I'll see many sales from the drinks and snacks. Everything should be easy-peasy. I can't wait for you to tell me all about the ride when you return."

As Debbie eyed Maurice and remembered the footprints outside the kitchen door, she hoped they wouldn't have too much to tell Paulette afterward.

CHAPTER FIFTEEN

*D*ebbie headed outside the café with her angel wings strapped on for the Christmas ride. The sun had set, and the crowd waited to climb aboard the train.

Kim, dressed to the nines in a gorgeous coat and matching hat, used a microphone to introduce the train personnel and the cast of actors. When she announced a special appearance by Maurice Devons, the audience burst into cheers and applause. Dressed in all black with his signature red boots, Maurice tipped his cowboy hat to the crowd and some of the women went wild, waving their mittened hands and begging for autographs.

Jude held a camera, squinting in the bright winter light. A few paces away, Victor took additional video of the crowd.

"Maurice!" one woman yelled as she pushed through the crowd to reach the star. "I'm such a huge fan. Will you take a selfie with me? Please?" When he chuckled, motioning her to come close, she dashed forward. "My girlfriends will be so jealous. You are so amazing."

He leaned in close to the woman as she held up her glittering phone to snap a picture.

"Maurice sure knows how to work the crowd," Janet said beside Debbie.

"He has a way with the women, no doubt. Is it any wonder his show is so popular?"

Jude cast a glance in Debbie's direction, indicating he had heard her. "I know a lot of people wish they could have the fans and the fame and money, but honestly, it can get tiring real fast. I can't tell you how many women have approached me to get close to Maurice. Despite what you might see on the outside, Maurice says he's sick of it all. He'd rather collect and repurpose antiques, but here we are."

"That's a shame," Debbie said. "For both of you. I like my life quiet and peaceful, surrounded by my family and friends."

Jude's expression shuttered as he fiddled with the lens of his camera. "Being around friends all day sounds amazing. I think you have the ideal life, Debbie."

Me too.

Jude waved at her and strode away to catch an impromptu caroling session with the crowd on the platform. His fellow cameraman, Victor, followed.

Already, the parking lot was full. Inside the café, Paulette served hot cocoa and cider to guests. She also handed out vanilla sugar cookies, gingerbread men, chocolate dipped pretzels, and plenty of stout candy canes. A steady stream of customers entered the café, eager to get something hot to drink as the temperatures fell.

In the meantime, children milled about near the fenced area of the live Nativity. Three woolly sheep and the donkey held court to the eager hands reaching out to pet a velvet nose. Tim had installed a hand sanitizer station inside the café for the kids to clean their hands, which Debbie was sure parents appreciated. She was also amused to see that the donkey that had caused Brad so much trouble that afternoon did, in fact, seem to enjoy the children's attention.

There was another attraction she hadn't considered. Crosby, Harry's dog, frolicked through the petting zoo area, barking with sheer excitement. Normally, Crosby didn't bark unless something warranted a warning, but today, his short tail wagged nonstop with exuberance.

When the sheep began to get nervous about Crosby's antics, Harry called, "Crosby, that's enough. Quiet now."

Crosby immediately fell silent but continued to prance around, making the children giggle with delight.

"Crosby is as big a hit as the sheep," Debbie said to Harry.

Harry laughed and folded his arms across his chest. His wise-man costume featured an elegant green turban with gold bro-cade and a glittering robe. "It doesn't surprise me, honestly. Crosby's always been a people person, and young people are his favorite."

"After you, of course," Debbie said. "He'll keep Paulette company at the café while we're on the train, right? We can take him inside if you like. Paulette will keep an eye on him."

"Thank you." Harry whistled. Crosby ran to Harry, his pink tongue lolling at the side of his mouth.

Debbie greeted the friendly dog, then led both Crosby and Harry into the café. "Can Crosby have a warm spot near the counter?" she called to Paulette.

"Yes, I have the perfect place for him," Paulette said as she handed a cup of frothy hot chocolate to a guest. "I'm sure things will quiet down with so many planning to go on the Christmas ride."

Leaving Harry to get Crosby settled, Debbie slipped out of the station to find her friends. Some of the *Days of Yesteryear* crew exited the café behind her. Debbie noticed Jude and Victor at the edge of the crowd, both men filming.

Jude waved at Debbie as she passed him. "Break a leg," he called out with a grin.

"Don't say that!" A laugh bubbled out of Debbie as she shook a finger at him. "Aren't you coming too?"

"No, someone's got to take adorable shots of the donkey and the train leaving the station. It's going to be the prettiest footage you ever saw. We are going to put you on the map, Debbie Albright. Don't you worry."

"Good luck then." She smiled.

Jude stopped midstep. "Hey, maybe I shouldn't ask this, but did that Leo and his brother patch things up? I felt bad being caught in the middle of their tiff at the café the other evening."

"Leo is Ricky's cousin," she corrected. "I don't know what will happen between them. I'm hoping for some Christmas cheer and grace for everyone. See you soon."

He waved. "Have a great ride."

Maurice and the other *Days of Yesteryear* team entered the train first, followed by Debbie and the cast of actors.

"I hear Leo Carosi is back in town," she overheard someone say. "How long has it been since he ran the trains?"

The voice faded as she climbed into the train car, followed by Harry, Brad, and Liza. The rest of the cast already waited inside.

"I can't believe how busy things are at the café. Is the train full?" Brad asked.

"I heard every seat has been taken," Liza replied as she adjusted her blue veil.

"It's great to be on TV. The Whistle Stop Café is going to be famous. Think you might need an extra cook?" Brad asked Debbie.

She beamed at him. "We're definitely busy. Busier than I can remember in a long while."

He grinned. "I'd love a shot to be a proper chef. No soup and sandwiches for me. Maybe I could turn the Whistle Stop Café into a steakhouse or something even bigger."

Debbie angled herself sideways, trying to keep her wings from banging anyone in the face. "Maybe we can chat later. Right now, I want to focus on the play."

"Honestly, Brad, you need to work on your timing," Liza said. "Didn't you used to work for Ricky? What happened there?"

Brad snorted. "I tried. Ricky's not the easiest guy to learn from. He's difficult in the kitchen. I cut my losses when I realized I wouldn't get fair treatment."

"That doesn't sound like the Ricky I know," Liza responded firmly. "He's always been sweet to my family."

Good girl, Debbie thought as she hurried forward along the narrow aisle, not willing to eavesdrop on a conversation that was none of her business. Nor did she want to have a discussion at the moment with Brad about a potential job. The Whistle Stop Café was meant to be a café with cozy comfort foods and plenty of treats, and as long as she and Janet were at the helm, that was what it would remain.

Besides, Ricky was one of the kindest men she had ever met. Brad's gossip didn't sit well with her. She pushed his words from her mind, determined to concentrate on the play.

Debbie and her crew waited at the front car. They would move from car to car, performing their short play. Janet blew out a nervous breath as Debbie fidgeted with her sash. Everyone looked a little nervous, including Harry, who wet his lips. It was one thing to put on a play. It was another thing entirely to have it filmed.

A long whistle pierced the air, and the train jolted forward with a hiss.

Kim entered the passenger car in her glamorous coat. She removed it, revealing a glittering navy cocktail gown that flared out at the bottom. With a silver belt and her hair curled perfectly, she resembled a 1940s movie star. "Maurice is getting everything ready with the camera crew. I'll pass through and introduce you all. I want the shepherds to come out. Maurice's cameramen will be taking video from different seats. One of them will precede you as you walk down the aisle, so don't go too fast. Everyone relax and act natural. The more at ease we are, the better this will come out."

Time seemed to slow as Debbie, Janet, Greg, and the rest of the cast waited. Debbie noticed that Brad stayed far away from Ricky, but she refused to worry about his and Liza's conversation.

Debbie glanced at her watch. "It's time, folks. Let's go."

Greg and his sons headed to the passenger cars, Greg adjusting Julian's shepherd costume at the last second. Debbie and Janet followed the shepherds, Mary and Joseph, and the wise men.

Kim narrated the beginning of the Nativity, reading from Luke, chapter two. "'In those days Caesar Augustus issued a decree that a census should be taken of the entire Roman world.'"

Debbie's mind went blank when Maurice's cameraman crouched low to the floor with his heavy camera pressed against the side of his cheek. She found herself wishing Jude had been the on-board cameraman, sure his friendly countenance would have eased her nerves. On either side of the aisle, eager faces stared at her. Men and women of all ages waited with a breathless anticipation.

Maurice sat to the left, his gaze piercing as he scanned the car. He held up his hand, possibly directing one of the other cameramen to another position.

She couldn't think about the cameras capturing every single line on her forehead or stray hair zapped with static electricity. She had to focus on her lines.

Greg turned in the center of the aisle. She caught his blue-eyed gaze, calm and steady. He was always so reassuring, no matter what she encountered. Jaxon and Julian, with their eyes wide, appeared terrified, which worked for the role. Behind her, she heard the soft rustle of Janet's robe, her best friend always by her side. The rest of the cast, the whole car, waited for her declaration. But the presence of Greg, Janet, and other close friends bolstered her.

Debbie inhaled deeply and threw out her arms, the satiny fabric of her costume falling back. Her voice rang out loud and clear. "Do not be afraid. I bring you good news that will cause great joy for all the people. Today in the town of David a Savior has been born to you; He is the Messiah, the Lord. This will be a sign to you: You will find a baby wrapped in cloths and lying in a manger."

Kim, who stood at the far end of the car, continued, "'Suddenly a great company of the heavenly host appeared with the angel, praising God and saying—'"

A screech of brakes ripped through the air. The floor of the car tilted crazily under Debbie's feet, flinging her backward. Out of the

corner of her eye, she saw a glittering gold halo fly free as Janet top-
pled onto someone's lap.

Debbie knocked into something solid. Her breath left her lungs
in one great gush as a pair of strong arms looped about her waist.
She fell to the ground, cushioned by someone else while a horrible
shriek of the wheels scraping against the rail echoed over the
stunned passengers' cries.

"Debbie!" came the muffled cry beneath her. "Are you okay?"

She moved her head enough to see Greg's white face. Jaxon and
Julian had collapsed in the center aisle, their eyes bulging with
terror. She rolled off Greg as the car tilted further.

"Dad!" Julian reached for his father, who reached back.

Janet grabbed the top of the nearest seat.

Screams reverberated as the lights flickered. The train car
lurched off the rail and into the unknown.

CHAPTER SIXTEEN

Outside of Brisighella, Italy
December 4, 1943

Nico woke in a shadowed cave to the sounds of men snoring. A faint gray light filtered into the cave, highlighting the forlorn interior. He sat up on the damp ground, the thin blanket barely lending any comfort.

Yet gratitude swept through him all the same as he rubbed away the last vestiges of sleep from his eyes. Paolo had swiftly intervened when the other men had wanted to interrogate him. Did his surprising mercy count as a miracle too?

Nico shivered and drew his ragged coat closer as he recalled the conversation from the night before. Paolo wanted Nico to deliver more messages, even as everything in Nico urged him to rush back to Rome and ensure Sophia was safe.

But he knew without a doubt that Sophia would want him to help her brother. To help the *resistenza*.

Beside him was the leather satchel, restocked with the remaining posters and the Nativity painting. He folded his blanket and whispered a prayer for the safety of his elderly neighbor, for Sophia, and for Catalina, who had offered him a place at Christmas.

Then he thought of Alberto in America, who by now must have a house full of giggling children and tantalizing aromas from whatever homemade sauce simmered on the stove. Even on rations, he knew Alberto would find a way to make every meal feel decadent. Music from the record player—perhaps "Ava Maria" or "Silent Night"—would provide a soft background as the family gathered at the table, holding hands for a brief grace.

He swallowed hard against the lump rising in his throat. He hadn't enjoyed a proper Christmas in a very long while. The day Alberto left on the ship for the United States had changed everything. Now, his reality couldn't be more different from Alberto's.

Glancing around the cave as the sunlight cast a long shaft of light against the floor, Nico counted the men. Twenty-two. There were likely more stationed in different areas, based on the whispers he'd heard in the night after he went to bed.

His legs aching, he rose and stretched, then tiptoed past the sleeping bodies toward the entrance where he could breathe in fresh air. The view from the mountains did not disappoint. As he surveyed the land, he saw how far he had come. Yet, a trek to the village would at least be a good day's walk. Was this Francesco who would give him a ride Catalina's missing grandson, closer than she or Eva imagined? How many ordinary Italians were involved in the resistenza?

Nico's stomach clenched. Would Matteo put out a wanted poster of Nico? He hoped not. He was a nobody.

"You're not thinking of running, are you?" a low voice asked behind Nico.

He whirled around to see Paolo grin as he held out an envelope.

In the bright morning light, Nico had the opportunity to study Sophia's older brother. He had aged this past year, with fine lines etched into the bronzed skin around his eyes, mouth, and forehead. They did nothing to diminish the spark in Paolo's clear gaze.

"I'll leave for the village first thing this morning. After that, I must return to Rome," Nico said.

Paolo studied Nico. "And will you join the resistenza back in Rome?"

To enter the heart of the beast and do what Paolo did? Nico had wrestled with that question all through the night as he tossed and turned, no thanks to the pebbles poking through the thin blanket, nor to his rising anxiety at what he might encounter in the great city upon his return.

"My first concern is to get Sophia out of Rome," he said slowly. "I haven't decided what I'll do after that."

To Nico's surprise, Paolo laid a hand on his shoulder. "I won't lie to you. The other men in the cave wanted you gone. They said you were a traitor seeking to ensure my sympathy by pretending to care for my sister to extract information and betray our band of brothers."

Our band of brothers.

The term startled Nico. Was that how the men inside that cave saw each other? As family? As brothers?

"But I've decided to trust my sister. I know she's a good judge of character. Always has been."

"I'll deliver your message, but I can't promise anything beyond that," *Nico told him. He hardly knew what to do with the mercy Paolo extended.*

Paolo heaved a great breath. "Good. I fear my face is well known. I dare not risk my men either."

When Nico entered the cave to retrieve his satchel, he overheard the others whispering back and forth. Snatches of conversation drifted to him, claiming that the Allies pushed on closer to Rome. His heart stuttered at the idea of what lay in store for Sophia and his neighbor.

"Is it true that families are being pulled out of their homes and sent to the camps?" one man muttered. "Is it true that Paolo has plans to—"

The other man, balding with gaunt cheeks, interrupted while glancing over his shoulder. "Yes, but hush. We don't know if it's safe to discuss."

The voices dropped as Nico reached for his bag, his gaze averted even though his ears perked at the news. His cheeks burned as he mulled over the men's conversation. Of course no one trusted him enough to share the resistenza objectives. Nor could he blame them. But he couldn't help but wonder at what Paolo had planned.

And whether Nico himself could join their band of brothers.

CHAPTER SEVENTEEN

ebbie lay stunned on the floor of the train, her mind and body refusing to work. Someone sobbed in the otherwise quiet car. She saw Greg scoot over to grab Jaxon in a bear hug.

"Thank God you're safe," he murmured before pulling Julian into a fierce embrace. His gaze met Debbie's as she struggled to regain her bearings.

"Debbie, are you okay?" Greg asked as he released his sons.

"I'm fine," she croaked, but he scooted closer all the same, enveloping her in a hug despite the broken angel wings. She buried her face in his chest.

He pulled away enough to study her face. "Thank God," he murmured again. "I don't think I've ever been so frightened in all my life."

Her breath caught with his vulnerable admission as she hugged him back.

But the moans on both sides of the car stole her attention as they parted. A quick glance around the passenger car revealed alarmed passengers clinging to their seats. Tree branches scraped against the windows, scattering clumps of snow to the ground.

They shouldn't be so close to the trees. She staggered to her feet, horror dawning afresh when she realized the car had careened off the tracks.

Kim, who had fallen near Maurice Devons, rose to her feet with him offering a hand. His Stetson had fallen off, and the camera crew groped around the floor for their equipment.

Dimly, she heard Maurice ask his cameraman, "Did you drop the camera?"

Kim stumbled toward Debbie. "I don't know what just happened, but we're going to need a first aid kit. Can you help me check for injuries?"

One of the conductors hunted for medical supplies while Kim and Debbie went row by row, asking if anyone needed help. When Debbie came across Janet, she helped her rise.

"Tell me I'm dreaming," her friend said.

"You're not," Greg said from behind Debbie. "We must have hit something and derailed."

Debbie found a woman with a cut on her forehead. "I need a bandage."

The conductor brought her the first aid kit. Debbie cleaned the scratch with an antiseptic wipe and covered it with a bandage, the pungent smell of the alcohol wipe clearing her senses.

"We need to get everyone off the train," the conductor informed Kim. "It's not safe to stay here."

Kim raised her hand to still the soft murmurs around her. "Listen up, everyone. It appears the train has gone off the tracks. We'll make some calls to get transportation to pick us up, but so far, it appears we're in the middle of the country. I need you all to work with us to stay calm, which will help make sure that no one else gets hurt. We're going to exit the train in an orderly fashion."

Debbie blew out a shuddering breath as she surveyed the passengers in the car.

"Debbie, are you sure you're okay?" Greg asked. "You're holding your wrist."

She glanced down, the shock beginning to wear off. Her wrist did indeed throb. "I might have a small sprain. I'll be fine until we get back to town." She started to shiver in spite of herself.

He frowned. "You're shaking. I'm going to get your coat." He hurried away.

"Thank you," Debbie told him, glad that she and the rest of the cast had stored their winter gear aboard the train before they'd changed into their costumes.

Jaxon and Julian huddled around her, and she tried to smile at them. "Are you guys okay?"

"Just rattled. Man, that was wild." But the lingering fear in Jaxon's eyes belied the bravado of his statement.

Janet approached Debbie, her gaze concerned. "I wonder how many cars came off the track."

"We'll get a better idea once we get off the train. Right now, I'm most concerned about getting everyone home safe and sound."

Janet shrugged out of her battered wings. "We had just passed the Millers' farm when everything went haywire. That's not too far outside of town. I think we could easily shuttle everyone back to town. I'm going to call Ian and let him know what happened. I don't want him to hear about it from someone else and worry."

Greg came with the coats slung over his arms, including Janet's. She gave him a grateful look when he handed it to her, then stepped away to make her call.

Greg helped Debbie remove her limp wings and bent halo, then shrug into her coat. "Are you sure you're okay?" he asked, a frown lining his forehead.

"Maybe I should ask you the same thing." She tried to joke and failed. "You're the one who cushioned me during the fall."

He gave her a lopsided smile.

Kim called out instructions for everyone to leave the train safely.

Debbie descended the narrow steps leading to the powdery ground with Greg and the boys. The stars in the night sky twinkled, and the moon shone bright enough to illuminate the snowbanks. It would have been a picturesque image if not for the air of catastrophe that hung over everything.

Leo stepped out of the control car and grimaced as he surveyed the wreckage. She pivoted to see what he was looking at as the gasps of the passengers filled the air.

The train had indeed jumped off the tracks, skidding into the enormous snowbank with two cars forming a V, like a toy train sent buckling off a wooden track.

"It's the engineer's fault!" a woman said loudly. "He was going way too fast, I tell you."

"I want a refund," another man snapped. "I planned on an exciting and memorable Christmas ride for the family, and this isn't exactly what I had in mind."

"Oh hush, George. You'll make the kids cry again," the petite woman beside him chided while her children crowded close.

Leo hurried across the snow to Debbie and Kim. "I promise you, I wasn't speeding. I don't know what happened, but it wasn't my fault."

"Did you hit a tree branch or something large enough to derail the train?" Greg asked.

Leo shook his head. "I would have seen something like that. Sometimes the tracks have fractures that can derail a train, but I thought these tracks would have been examined for that before we did this. I'm not certain, but I know I didn't see anything on the tracks to cause alarm. Is anyone hurt?"

"Nothing too serious." Kim held her phone to her ear. "I'm going to arrange rides back to the station."

Leo nodded, his expression worried, and he stepped away from Kim as Ricky descended the train, then helped Harry down. Brad and Liza followed with Janet.

"We'll need to start walking to the nearest farm." Kim called out. "We'll have vehicles coming soon to drive us to the station."

The crowd moved, trailing after Kim.

Debbie heard Maurice's voice over everyone else's. "Get those cameras rolling. I don't want to miss another minute of this surreal evening."

Debbie cringed. Was he planning to capitalize on the incident? That would hardly portray Dennison in a positive light.

Greg wrapped an arm around her, pulling her close to his side. "Are you in pain? Come on. Let's get you home."

"Home sounds wonderful," she said. "Greg, this is a disaster. Who's going to want to come to Dennison to ride the Christmas train after this?"

"I know," he said grimly. "We'll talk about it later. I'm just grateful you and the kids are safe."

She blew out a long breath that fogged in the chilly air, her shoulders slumping forward. His arm around her tightened, offering comfort. In all her adventures over this past year, Greg had proved to be constant, an encourager when she needed him the most.

"Thank you, Greg," she said. "I don't know what I would do without you. I never want to lose you."

The admission came out almost without her will, blurted partly because of the train derailing and the relief that everyone was safe.

He glanced at her, his mouth parting as if in wonder. "Debbie, I—" he said thickly.

"Almost at the farm!" Kim shouted from the head of the line. "Hang in there, everyone."

Debbie's cheeks heated when she glanced at Jaxon and Julian. It was unlikely they had heard her. Had it been rash of her to admit the depth of her feelings? She hoped she hadn't embarrassed Greg or his sons. Of course the boys knew she was dating their dad, but beyond that, nothing more had been said or promised. She had been so careful not to rush things. But she couldn't deny she wanted more. A lot more.

Did Greg feel the same way? Before she could ask, his phone vibrated. He answered immediately, and Debbie heard Paulette's frantic voice on the other end.

"I'm sorry, Mom. Yes, my text said we derailed. No, we're all fine. We're coming to the station soon. Please don't cry. No one is hurt. Only the train sustained damage, so you don't need to worry. No, we don't need to take the boys or Debbie to the hospital. Yes, I'm sure. It's going to be fine, Mom. I promise. See you soon. Yes, it's a miracle we're okay. Love you too. Bye."

When he ended the call, he wrapped his arm around Debbie and led her through the drifting snowbanks. "Mom will be better when she sees us come into the café with all our fingers and toes intact. Someone ran into the café and told her the train derailed, and then she got my text."

"We're all being a bit reactive right now," Debbie said quietly.

Maurice trudged past them, and Debbie noticed that he kept his gaze averted from her. The camera crew struggled to keep pace with him, while one of them filmed the crowd walking from the train. Surely Maurice wouldn't air the footage.

Would he?

Despite the earlier complaining, Harry started singing "O Come, All Ye Faithful," his rich voice carrying in the winter breeze. Before long, everyone joined in as they followed Kim to the nearby farm. Snow draped the rooftop of the gabled house, presenting a charming sight.

Laughter drifted, and the mood shifted to something almost sacred. Ahead, Janet waved at Greg and Debbie, her smile present despite all that had happened. "I think we should ensure that everyone gets an extra treat and a cup of cocoa after this ride."

"We absolutely should, especially after they graced us with that lovely carol." Debbie laughed. "It was wonderful, wasn't it?"

When the guests reached the farm site, cheers rose up. Other than a few scratches and scares, no one had been seriously hurt. Debbie breathed a prayer of gratitude for that.

She inhaled the crisp air, her pulse slowing as Greg helped her navigate the snowy path leading to the Miller farm. Jaxon and Julian stayed close as well, their cheeks rosy red with the cold.

The train had been too close a call. Too close a brush with danger.

She would never take the gift of being surrounded by safe, healthy loved ones for granted again.

An hour later, when Debbie stepped off the school bus at the station with Greg and the boys, chaos met them. The sheep wandered through the parking lot, bleating loudly, while the donkey trotted around the cars, eluding several men who slid around on the ice as they tried to recapture it. Children laughed as they pointed at the escaped animals. One waved a candy cane as if to coax the donkey closer.

"What on earth happened?" Janet cried as she reached Debbie's side.

"I don't know. How did the animals get loose?" Debbie scanned the parking lot. "What a nightmare."

"I'll help round up the sheep." Greg motioned for his sons to follow, and the three Connors trotted into the fray.

Paulette barged out of the café and made a beeline straight for Debbie. "The painting is missing!"

With a shout, Ricky plunged through the crowd, pushing his way into the café. Debbie and Janet dashed after him, skidding to a halt at the wall where the paintings and donated art remained on display. As Paulette had said, the place of honor was bare, the yellow wall a sharp contrast to the colorful paintings left behind.

"You didn't see or hear anything?" Ricky asked as he shoved a hand through his hair.

Paulette's chin trembled as if she might cry. "No, I didn't. I went into the kitchen to grab more treats for the display case before the guests returned. Someone ran into the café and yelled about the train derailing, so I checked my phone and saw a text from Greg about it. I called him to see if everyone was okay. While I was on the phone, I heard Crosby bark out in the café. I tried to go see what was bothering him, but the door wouldn't move. Someone had blocked it with a table. By the time I got around the back and in through the front door, the painting and whoever took it were gone. I'm so sorry."

A shout came from outside the café, drawing everyone's attention to the window.

Tim, Brad's dad, ran across the slick ice of the parking lot, sliding and flailing. "Grab that donkey!" he shouted to the crowd.

Greg dodged left toward the ornery beast while Brad lunged forward, his face a mask of concentration. The crowd standing around cheered—which made the donkey all the more excited as it scrambled on the ice.

Several men in the crowd fanned out, arms wide as they tried to make a barrier to catch the runaway donkey.

"Weren't the animals secured in a fence?" Debbie asked.

"Yes, they were. I'm not sure what happened." Paulette frowned. "Maybe too many little kids pressed against the pen and something got jostled loose." She sniffled, her eyes filling. "Forgive me, I'm so stressed over that painting and the derailment."

"Go sit down, Paulette. You deserve a break." Janet brought her phone up to her ear and stepped away from the group, probably to speak with Ian again.

Ricky was pacing back and forth in front of the spot on the gallery wall. "Surely someone must have seen the person who took the painting."

Paulette hugged herself as she sank into one of the café chairs. "I don't know who might have come in or out while I was on the phone with Greg. The door was unlocked so that guests could warm up in here if they needed to, but not many did. Someone wanted to keep me in the kitchen while he or she took the painting."

The conversation stopped as Maurice came into the café. He tipped his hat back, his eyes bright with excitement. "Where's Jude? Has anyone seen my cameraman?"

Debbie pointed to the window. "He's outside with the rest of the crew. They're all trying to catch the donkey, or at least get some video."

"Good man," Maurice said under his breath. "I hope he's getting every single second of this day."

"Please tell me you're not going to air footage of the train derailment," Debbie said as she tried to breathe calmly.

Maurice raised an eyebrow. "Come on, Debbie. People love drama. It skyrockets the ratings. I'm going to have the best show of my entire career."

Crosby whined.

Harry led him to the door and let him out. "Go help, Crosby. See if you can round up the sheep and donkey."

Crosby bounded across the parking lot up to the rebellious donkey. The dog danced around Burro, herding him back to the men and Brad, who waited with a rope.

A yelp of triumph burst from Brad as he lassoed the donkey and hauled him to the pen. Before long, the sheep joined Burro, and Tim secured the gate.

Debbie exhaled with relief while the crowd outside cheered. Then she asked Maurice, "Are you aware the Nativity painting went missing today?"

He gaped at her. "What? No." He spun to face the wall as if to check for himself. "What on earth?"

"Paulette was in the kitchen when the theft happened."

He drew up to his full height. "This is terrible. Who would do something so awful?"

You, perhaps? She nearly blurted out the words, but held back. Her expression, however, must have betrayed her racing thoughts.

"You don't think I had something to do with this, do you?" he protested, pointing to his own chest. "I was with you on the train, after all. Nearly losing my life along with everyone else on board, I might add. I may have wanted that painting for the show, but I'm not a thief. No sir."

Ricky edged closer to Debbie. "You really pressured me to sell it the other day. Maybe you know something about the painting that Debbie and I don't, something that would make it worth stealing when I wouldn't sell."

Maurice yanked the brim of his hat lower, the muscle in his jaw flexing. "I've got nothing to hide. I made you a private offer. A very decent and respectful offer, if I recall. Why throw my generosity back in my face?"

Ricky's lips curled into a snarl. "An offer I refused. Besides, filming our train wreck is hardly respectful."

Debbie stepped between the two men. Ricky had just endured a train derailment and the loss of a beloved family painting. She could hardly blame him for his anger, but she didn't want him to get into trouble. "We'll sort this out. It's been a very trying day for all of us, and we'll think more clearly in the morning. Ricky, why not take your wife home?"

Ricky glared at Maurice. "All right, I'll get my family and go. But don't you think about leaving town."

Maurice's mouth dropped open. "I beg your pardon?"

"You heard me," Ricky replied coldly. Without another word, he left.

"When do you intend to leave Dennison?" Debbie asked Maurice.

"Later this week. I don't have any reason to stay longer than that." Maurice scowled. "I've got staff itching to go home to their families for the holiday. I've kept them long enough as it is. Regardless of what you might think, I'm not your villain, Debbie." He stalked out of the café.

Janet rejoined them. "Ian is coming to investigate the theft. I overheard Ricky and Maurice. They both sounded angry."

"Maurice offered to buy the painting the other day, but Ricky refused," Debbie explained. "It seems Ricky believes Maurice decided to acquire the painting through a less savory method."

Janet whistled, long and low. "We're all wound up right now. I can't blame Ricky for getting heated."

Paulette offered to start closing shop. The crowd outside began to disperse, but a few wandered into the café for one last cup of cocoa.

Kim was nowhere to be seen. Neither was Leo. Greg, Jaxon, and Julian entered the café, their cheeks pink from the cold and the exertion of wrangling the animals. Debbie headed to the display case to get some cookies to send home with them. She'd likely take a few home herself. Everyone could use the comfort food.

When she handed the bag to Greg, she explained about the missing painting.

Greg took the bag and gave it to Jaxon. "What a strange coincidence. I just heard from Tim that the rope securing the animal pen was loosened, which is how they escaped. Feels kind of bizarre, doesn't it?"

A chill swept through her as her gaze collided with his.

"What did you say?" Janet demanded. "What do you mean, loosened?"

"He thinks the pen was tampered with," Greg said slowly. "Someone wanted the animals to get loose."

CHAPTER EIGHTEEN

Outside of Brisighella, Italy
December 4, 1943

Later that morning, Nico slung the satchel over his shoulder. Snow fell outside the cave, coating the ground in a thin layer of white. Already, he felt the chill of the mountains where the wind sliced through his threadbare clothes. The men of the resistenza watched his descent from the cave toward the remains of a faint path to the road, where he would meet the driver.

He heard the crunching of boots behind him and whirled to see Paolo catching up with him. Paolo said nothing as they headed down the rugged terrain together. A heaviness weighed in the chilled air, as if in silent warning to fulfill the task and somehow pass the test.

Nico raised his hand in farewell to the other men. No one waved back.

This winter weather was all bite and no cheer, yet he had never felt more alive or more aware of his surroundings. A curious freedom resided within the mountains, unlike the claustrophobic press of the city. Danger waited here, yes, but it didn't bother him quite so much. Something had happened to him. It was as if the tethers of Rome, of the Party, of Matteo and Captain Accardo had snapped one by one, leaving him less encumbered. Less afraid.

One last string remained. The one that truly mattered. The one binding him to Sophia.

He and Paolo had walked about half a mile when the low rumble of a truck came from behind them. Nico turned to see an old jalopy come to a grinding halt.

A young man stuck his head out the window, grinning from ear to ear. His black hair, in need of a haircut, blew about his forehead. "Need a ride into a town, Paolo?"

Was this the driver Paolo had promised?

"Not me," *Paolo answered.* "You know I'm too much trouble for your village, but I've brought a friend. His name is Nico. He needs to see our postmaster."

The man inside the truck flashed a smile. "I'm Francesco. My nonna has a farm outside the village."

So he was that Francesco, whose white-haired grandmother, Catalina, had told Nico he would be welcome at her table at Christmas. The same Francesco ran errands for Paolo.

Still, Nico's tongue refused to work.

*"You needn't stare at me as if I've sprouted horns."
Francesco shot Nico a grin. "Get in before you waste
the morning and my gas. You'll need to get to the post
office before it closes, and you'll never make it on foot."*

*Nico did as he was told, climbing into the truck
from the other side. He fingered the slip of paper in his
pants pocket, the message rolled tightly.*

*"Keep an eye on him, will you?" Paolo thrust sev-
eral filthy bills through the open window.*

*"No problem. I've got a few supplies in the back of
the truck for you. Take what you need," Francesco said
to Paolo, who eagerly headed to the truck bed to grab
two burlap bags.*

*When Paolo had the bags, Francesco released the
brake, and the truck jolted forward, leaving Sophia's
brother behind.*

*Questions flooded Nico's mind. He wondered how
the men had met and how long Francesco had worked
for the resistenza. He chose not to ask. Knowing less
seemed prudent somehow. As the truck rumbled into
the small village where everyone had rejected his
request for a bed for the night, he noticed several Nazi
soldiers entering a building.*

Francesco growled, making his feelings for the invading army abundantly clear. "The Germans are here sooner than we anticipated. Paolo won't like this one bit." Still, Francesco drove boldly into town, raising a hand in greeting as they passed villagers and soldiers alike.

"The Allies are making progress toward Rome," Nico murmured. He hardly dared look out his window, afraid to catch some gray uniformed soldier's probing stare.

"We Italians will be crushed between the armies like grapes in a winepress." Francesco parked at the post office. "Do what you must and be quick about it."

Nico pulled out his most garish poster, stalked to the post office, and flung the door open. He pinned each of the four corners on a corkboard, Il Duce staring at him. One Nazi soldier entered the post office and watched Nico, grunting when Nico stepped back from his work.

The postmaster—Salvatore Rossi, according to Paolo—waited behind a grill in a shadowed room, his gaze blank.

How could Nico ask the man about a telegram as Paolo had ordered while a German soldier stood so close? How would he slip Paolo's message to the postmaster?

"Can I help you?" the postmaster inquired, his tone bored. He appeared old and tired, with thin strands of hair carefully combed over a balding dome. But his narrow eyes were sharp, following the German's movements.

"Yes. Can you tell me how much it costs to send a telegram?" Nico leaned in until his forehead nearly touched the metal grill separating them. "Paolo recommended you."

The old man's eyes flickered, yet he merely shrugged as if unimpressed with Nico's claim. "Everyone recommends me these days. Will you write your message down?"

"I already have." He pulled out the tightly rolled slip and slid it across to the man.

At that moment, Francesco sauntered into the post office, offering a casual nod of recognition to the German soldier, who inspected the Mussolini poster.

The soldier must have been satisfied with what he saw. He brushed past Francesco and headed outside. Nico and Mr. Rossi exhaled at the same time. The postmaster tucked the slip of paper into his sleeve as Francesco reached the grill.

Mr. Rossi slid a different slip of paper under the grill but didn't let it go. "I want Francesco to have the latest message. I know him. I don't know you, even if you claim to know Paolo."

"I understand."

Francesco tucked the note into his pocket.

"Good day, gentlemen." Salvatore Rossi nodded curtly then turned away and began to shuffle papers, signaling the interaction over. "Tell Paolo he is entirely too trusting."

They exited the post office, heading out into the winter wind.

"Is that it for the errands?" Francesco asked as he shoved his hands into his pockets.

"I believe so." Nico's skin prickled when he spotted the same Nazi soldier from the post office outside on the street. The blond man appeared uninterested, but Nico couldn't help but suspect that the soldier was monitoring them.

"How about a trip to the market?" Francesco offered as he ambled across the street to his truck. "I have some goods to sell. It's not the easiest way to get rich, but nothing beats the farm life."

Nico suspected the resistenza band remained fed thanks to the efforts of Francesco and his family. "I met your grandmother. And her feisty daughter."

"My mother?" Francesco huffed a laugh as he hopped into his truck, clearly unfazed by the sight of *men in gray uniforms marching down the street. "She is as fierce as she seems. Her bark matches her bite, but she has a good heart."*

"I'm grateful for your grandmother's hospitality. No one would let me stay the night here. I couldn't even find a barn, except for your family's stable."

Francesco smiled, though it appeared somewhat strained, as he started the engine. The truck rattled to life—a comforting sound among so many gray uniforms. Yet for all the danger outside, Francesco's voice remained even. "It's what my family does, Nico. Along with Paolo. My mother hates to take risks these days, probably because she wants to keep everyone safe. But not my nonna. She believes that if we lose our humanity during the dark times, including the ability to care about others and to serve as needed, then we are truly lost."

Nico's chest tightened as the truck backed into the street. A child darted past, chased by a thin puppy, and a woman followed close behind. Innocent people with much to lose now that the Italian King, Victor Emmanuel III, had declared war against Hitler. Indeed, the very country felt as if it were being ripped apart as Mussolini and Hitler dug in for the battle of a lifetime in their quest to control Italy and the rest of the world.

A long breath escaped Nico as they drove away from the post office. He twisted in his seat to see through the back window of the truck. Armored German vehicles drove down the main street. It was a familiar sight in Rome, but he doubted that was the case here. The German army was advancing to meet the Allies. Perhaps they would turn Brisighella into another Winter Line to prevent the British and Americans from descending from the north.

Would he be able to leave the mountains after all? And would Paolo's secret message, now in the custody of the postmaster, be too late?

CHAPTER NINETEEN

Debbie sat at a café table with her mother, Paulette, and Janet, the café closed and locked after most of the crowd had left. Debbie had insisted that Greg go home. Surely the boys needed a good supper and rest. Greg tried to talk her into leaving the café too, but she couldn't yet. Not when she felt so responsible for Ricky's missing painting.

Mom put an arm around Debbie. "My poor girl. I can't believe you went through such an ordeal today. Is there no word on what might have happened to the painting?"

Debbie shook her head. "Maybe the security camera caught something."

"How did Ricky take the news?"

"Not well. He seems wound up, but he's holding it together. When Maurice came into the café, practically glowing because he got some exciting footage, I was afraid for a second that Ricky might hit him."

"Do you think there's a chance Maurice or one of the riders will threaten to sue for such a wild ride?" Debbie's mom asked.

Debbie shuddered. "Let's hope that doesn't happen. At least no one was seriously injured."

Kim pushed open the door to the café, her shoulders slumped. "Got any coffee or snacks? I don't need the sugar, but my mood sure wants comfort food."

"I think we have a few scones left," Debbie said. "Cinnamon raisin, which is practically health food."

"The perfect pick-me-up," Kim said, and given her drawn features, it seemed the director could use it.

"Do you know what happened, Kim?" Janet asked as she patted the seat beside her for their friend. "I haven't heard much from Ian. He wanted to check on me first, but I told him he better get out to the crash site before the weather compromised it more than it already has."

Kim removed her coat and sank into the chair beside Janet. "I have no idea what caused the accident. Or the theft. Leo's a nervous wreck, insisting that nothing happened to cause the train to jump the tracks the way it did. He's terrified we'll accuse him of speeding. Of course, we'll need to get an inspection of the tracks to see if there are cracks. Leo insists the rails were clear. Otherwise, I don't know what to say."

"Did you look at the security camera footage?" Debbie asked.

"I didn't get a chance to before an officer came and took it away as evidence."

"I wonder if the back door rattling to the kitchen might have been someone trying to sneak into the café," Debbie murmured.

"Could be," Janet said.

Debbie brought the scone to Kim, along with a cup of the stoutest leftover coffee possible. "Sorry, bottom of the pot. It's going to be pretty burnt at this point."

Kim waved a dismissive hand. "I'll take it. I have a splitting headache. Honestly, I'm terrified that if word gets out that the train is unsafe, we'll lose our tourists and maybe even some grants."

"I've read about train derailments," Janet said slowly. "There are about three a day, though only a few make the news. Some are worse than others. At least today, everyone walked away from the accident, safe and sound. Maybe it was just something to do with the rails needing maintenance. Is the station responsible for that?"

"The railroad lines must comply with safety regulations. If a track falls short, the railroad must either repair the issue or slow the trains. Or even remove the track altogether." Kim picked up the scone but set it down again as if her appetite had fled. "I can't even begin to imagine the cost of replacing or repairing our train. These were historic cars too. Very difficult to replace."

Janet frowned. "Does a train have a black box or something similar?"

"There are cameras," Kim said wearily. "We can check those. I've never known Leo to make a mistake. He doesn't take careless risks with people's lives. Back in 1947, the Interstate Commerce Commission issued the speed limit orders following a terrible crash in 1946 near Naperville, Illinois. An Exposition Flyer rammed into an Advance Flyer at eighty miles an hour. It was devastating for all involved and changed the railroad system for good."

"You all are lucky you walked away from this," Paulette said.

"Not lucky," Debbie corrected. "Perhaps we were more protected than we realized. A Christmas miracle, if you will."

"Christmas angels?" Debbie's mom offered with a trembling smile.

"It sure beats Christmas ghosts," Debbie replied.

A police car pulled up to the café. Ian got out of the car, sharp in his uniform. Moments later, he came through the café door, greeting the women with a somber expression. Dark circles shadowed his eyes, evidence of his nasty cold. "If you don't mind, I'll keep my distance from the rest of you, still being sick and all."

"Poor guy," Debbie murmured.

Janet rose and soon returned with a small teapot, a cup, and an assortment of teas for her husband to choose from. Her tray also held honey and lemon—a care package for what ailed him.

Ian sank down at a small table, keeping ample space between himself and the others. "Thank you, Janet." He gave her a smile before seeing to the steaming pot of hot water in front of him. "I need to chat with Leo Carosi further. I'm not an expert, but I couldn't find anything wrong with the rails. No blockage, like a fallen tree. My deputies are viewing the footage from the train. If anything, my guess is that Leo's skill kept the train from worse damage. Deputy Vaughn suggested checking the spot where the trains switch tracks."

"You mean the railway switch and crossings?" Kim asked, her frown deepening.

"Right." He sipped his tea, swallowing on a sigh of comfort. "Leo suggested that it's not uncommon for snow and ice to prevent the proper movement of switch rails."

"Weather could be the cause," Kim said. "Many of the older stations have employees to keep the railroad switches clear of snow and ice, especially ones with limited-use trains like ours. I'll check with the staff to see if someone neglected their duties. It's not uncommon for trains to have trouble maintaining speed on icy tracks."

"Someone was out by the railway switch," Ian said. "I saw prints in the snow, Kim."

The museum director paused. "Well, it didn't snow today. It snowed last night, so those prints could have been from early this morning when someone from my staff checked the tracks prior to the train running. Leonard Markham usually switches the train tracks the morning of a train ride. I'll speak with him to find out more."

"I wouldn't mind speaking with him as well. I saw footprints walking back and forth to and from the switch. I snapped a photo of the boot treads." Ian pulled out his phone to show them. "Sorry, these photos aren't the best quality, but the prints should still be visible."

Several distinct footprints were imprinted in the snow.

Debbie leaned back against the seat. "We've got a missing painting, an obnoxious online celebrity, a big crowd of newcomers desperate to see Maurice Devons, a few runaway sheep, and an escaped donkey. Which leaves us with what, other than a day of pure chaos?"

Kim pressed her lips together. "I'll be conducting interviews as soon as possible. I'd like to think our accident was due to the weather and nothing more. But after all the investigating you two have done so far in Dennison, I've learned not to jump to conclusions. Better to gather all the facts first. We must figure out what happened before the depot's reputation is ruined."

"Here's hoping no one sues," Janet added.

"I brought the footage from the café to show you," Ian said. "Maybe something one of you sees could help us learn something valuable."

"Of course." Kim rose from the table. She swayed for a moment, catching herself by grabbing onto a chair.

"Are you dizzy?" Debbie stood to support her.

"I might have hit my head," Kim answered as she rubbed her temples.

"You should get that checked out."

"I'll have Barry drive me to the hospital after Ian has a chance to view the tapes," Kim assured them. "I'm curious to see if he can shed some light on this."

Debbie, Kim, and Janet accompanied Ian to Kim's office. Debbie's mom decided to go home, pausing to press a kiss to Debbie's cheek. "I'm glad you're okay, honey. I love you." Paulette left as well.

Ian sat down at Kim's computer and inserted a thumb drive. He let Kim navigate to the right app and then took over. He brought up the view of the café and navigated to the hour the train had derailed. A grainy feed displayed a view of the café interior. Crosby lay with his head on his paws next to the display case. Paulette wiped down the counter and then emptied a new roll of quarters into the cash register. Then an older woman ran into the café, waving her arms. Paulette reached into her apron and pulled out her cell phone. The woman left while Paulette gazed at her phone. She tapped the screen and held it to her ear.

"That must be when Paulette learned about the train derailment. Then she received the text from Greg," Debbie said. "He texted her as soon as he got off the train. She called as we were walking to the Millers' farm."

On the screen, Paulette entered the kitchen, the phone pressed against her ear. Crosby lay quietly, his eyes closed as if peacefully asleep.

"I don't see anyone else in the café," Kim said as she leaned in closer to the screen. "Am I missing something? Didn't Paulette say someone pushed a table against the door to the kitchen and Crosby barked?"

"She did," Debbie admitted. "I don't see anyone barricading Paulette in the kitchen."

The feed remained the same...until Crosby raised his head, sniffing the air. He jumped to his feet, barking, his tail wagging furiously. The camera captured the top edge of the café door bursting open, and a table went skidding across the floor.

"Crosby saw something," Ian muttered as he stopped the footage and rewound it. "And there's our mysterious table against the kitchen door."

Debbie watched the feed play out a second time, right up to the point where Paulette ran to Crosby from the front entrance, stooping to pet him and calm him. But Crosby refused, standing alert, his tail straight up.

He had seen something. The question was, what? No one had approached the café counter in that time frame.

"None of what you mentioned explains our missing painting," Janet protested as she stepped back from the screen to glance at her husband. "And did someone tamper with the camera? It should be pointed at the door of the café."

"Someone must have moved it," Debbie said.

Kim's eyes widened. "Yes, Barry said it looked different the other day. I brushed him off."

Ian appeared deep in thought, rubbing his chin. He took a rattling breath, reminding Debbie that Dennison's police chief remained under the weather and likely needed more of Janet's chicken noodle soup. Not to mention rest.

"Someone, seeing an opportunity with only Crosby as a witness, snatched the painting. Who, how, and when?" Ian said finally. "I'm going to have to open a criminal investigation to get some answers. There weren't that many people at the station at the time of the robbery. Otherwise..."

"Christmas ghosts," Debbie said under her breath.

CHAPTER TWENTY

*L*ater that evening, the sky glittered with countless stars as Debbie parked in front of her charming craftsman house. She sat in the warmth of her car, a headache mounting. Outside, the colorful lights strung about her porch flickered on, bathing the snow in hues of red and blue and green. She had chosen colored lights this year as a nod to her childhood. Greg had helped her put them up before the weather had taken a turn for the worse.

She rested her head on the steering wheel and groaned out loud. How could the perfect holiday unravel faster than a ball of yarn batted around by a rambunctious kitten? She sent up a prayer for a miracle as she made herself move and collect her bags. Now that the day had ended, she ached all over. When she unlocked the door to her house, she breathed a sigh of relief. Discarding her coat and boots, she sent out several texts to check up on her friends, starting with Kim.

I'm on my way to the hospital, Kim texted back. Barry's worried about a concussion. I'm too tired to argue with him. If you need me, I'll be at the ER. Can't stand that place.

Debbie grinned despite her worry over Kim. Barry wouldn't let any harm come to his wife.

Let me know the results, Debbie replied. By the way, any news on Leonard Markham and the rail switch?

Kim's reply appeared quickly for how long it was. HE SAID HE WENT OUT TO THE SWITCH AT THE CRACK OF DAWN AND CLEARED THE ICE AND SNOW. I BELIEVE HIM. HE'S A RELIABLE EMPLOYEE WHO ALWAYS DOUBLE-CHECKS HIS WORK. HE TAKES SAFETY SERIOUSLY. BOTH HE AND LEO ARE SICK WITH WORRY THAT THE TOWN WILL BLAME THEM FOR THE ACCIDENT. I FEEL SO BAD FOR LEONARD. WE'VE GOT TO WORK OUT WHAT HAPPENED, AND SOON.

I AGREE, Debbie answered.

She checked in with Janet, who reported that she and Ian were taking it easy and planned to go to bed early.

As for Greg, Debbie decided she would rather hear his voice. She was about to dial his number when her phone vibrated in her palm. The glowing screen showed Greg's name.

She smiled as she answered. "I was just about to call you."

"I wondered if you wanted me to drop anything off there for you? Food, sugar, anything?"

His care was so consistent. She loved how he thought of the little details in serving others.

"You're so thoughtful. Janet sent me home with leftover ravioli soup from the café. I'm going to reheat it for supper," she assured him. "As for sugar, I'm saving the calories for Christmas dinner. Oh, who am I kidding? I've been sampling the cookies at work."

"Ah, I can't blame you." He cleared his throat with a chuckle. "And your wrist?"

"I forgot all about my wrist when Ian came to the café to tell us what he'd discovered about the train."

"Oh? Was he able to give you any answers?"

"It's hard to say right now what happened. But Ian thinks it's possible that someone switched the train tracks. He saw several prints in the snow. Leonard Markham is usually the one to maintain the tracks, but it sounds like he didn't do anything that would push the switch lever in the wrong direction. In the meantime, Kim's getting the cameras assessed on the train to clear Leo's name. She believes him when he said he wasn't speeding."

"Good."

"Ian also checked the security footage of the café. We found nothing, Greg. Crosby got excited, but the camera didn't show anyone coming into the café. Someone angled it away from the door."

"That's unfortunate."

She removed the container of soup from the paper bag while holding the phone between her shoulder and ear. "Right?" Then she lowered her voice, admitting what she actually feared—an occurrence that seemed to happen more as she sought Greg's advice and grew to trust it. "Honestly, I'm wondering about Maurice. Ricky said that Maurice pressured him to sell the painting, and he was pushy with me about it too. Could Maurice be a likely suspect?"

"He was with us on the train," Greg pointed out. "Who else would want the painting?"

"Leo wants the painting because he's jealous that his cousin Ricky got both it and the restaurant when their grandfather died. But he was on the train too. He or Maurice must have had help. Would anyone else want to hurt Ricky?"

Greg cleared his throat. "Yes, but he was on the train too. I overheard Brad saying some unkind things about Ricky when the boys and I first came to the café today. I didn't ask for clarification, but Brad sure doesn't have much love for the guy. He seems intent on tarnishing Ricky's reputation."

"I overheard him doing that as well. Brad might be full of hot air, but you're right that he's been near us, thanks to the play. I don't think it's him."

"I agree. I spoke with Tim about the animals getting out. He was pretty angry that someone had endangered Burro and the sheep. He said he was outside the entire time, talking to the guests who weren't on the train. He and many of the guests in the parking lot were so frantic about the train accident that he missed whoever let the farm animals loose. He was desperate to get in touch with his son," Greg said.

"Understandably," Debbie murmured, remembering how frantic Greg had been to check on the boys.

"And you have the crew of *Days of Yesteryear*," Greg added. "Anyone could have had access to an open café. Who wanted the painting the most?"

The microwave beeped, letting Debbie know it had finished reheating her soup. The aroma of the tomatoes made her mouth water as she pulled the steaming bowl out of the microwave.

"Other than Maurice, Leo, and perhaps some stranger who secretly loves Nativity paintings, your guess is as good as mine," she told Greg. "And that's not the only mystery I need to unravel. I've found hardly any leads on Ricky's uncle, Nico. It's as if the guy disappeared after World War II. Did your family ever hear about Alberto receiving a painting from Italy?"

"I'd have to check into that," Greg said. "I do remember hearing about Ricky's difficult relationship with his cousin. It's been that way for many years now, unfortunately. Leo ran the train for several years before retiring. Without any trouble, I might add."

"Leo resents losing the restaurant and painting to Ricky, like I said. Ricky said Leo received investments, but you know how wills can complicate lives."

"I can guess," Greg replied. "If Leo felt cheated, then perhaps he had some motivation to want that painting back."

"We'd have not one suspect but two," Debbie said as she fished for a spoon from her cutlery drawer. "Leo plus another suspect working together to steal the painting. And then there's the derailment. Ian said he found several different sets of tracks leading to the switch. The station staff makes sure the switches are cleared of snow and ice before the train heads out on the track. Did the switch get jammed with ice and no one noticed? Or was it deliberately tampered with?"

"I'm afraid we can't know that until we learn more," Greg said. "Be careful, Debbie. Something doesn't feel right about all of this. I don't want to see you get hurt."

She had to laugh. "How would I get hurt?"

There was no amusement in his tone. "If someone isn't afraid to derail a train full of passengers, what makes you think they'll stop shy of hurting a single woman?"

Her laughter faded. She couldn't argue with that.

CHAPTER TWENTY-ONE

The unrelenting gray dome of sky promised more flakes and a very cold night in the cave when Nico returned to the mountains with Francesco.

Supplies proved nearly impossible to procure despite the trip to the farmers market. Following their ill success, Francesco showed Nico where to find a small black market tucked between two seedy shops. Nico's enthusiasm soon faded when he learned of the prices for basic supplies. No meat could be found anywhere. No one had salt on hand, since nearly all of it had been confiscated for the Nazis. The herbs and spices his nonna had used so freely were all but gone. Even the scraps of metal to be found within a kitchen drawer had long since been melted and delivered to the new Roman Empire.

While Francesco haggled over the price of two bags of rice—the rations likely stolen for the purpose of resale on the black market—Nico scanned the street for danger. Instead of the prosperity, safety, and national pride that had been apparent during his childhood, he saw starving faces and bowed shoulders.

"You look angry," Francesco said to him. "You should be. At least we'll be fed tonight, but as for the others?" He gestured to the milling crowd in the market. "Some won't be so fortunate."

They left the shop, and Nico carried one of the bags of rice, a triumph considering the sheer rush of villagers seeking additional food. Rations continued to shrivel. Food was scarce for all. Bread would have been wonderful, but such luxuries were nearly nonexistent these days. Meat too, unless someone killed a beloved farm animal that provided other food. He tried not to shudder when he overheard one villager discuss taking the rocks near the train tracks to soak in water and somehow make a salt-like substitute liquid to season meals. The very idea made him nauseated. Yet everyone had to improvise the best he or she could to survive.

In Rome, the orti di guerra, the war gardens, took up space in the city parks and the sports fields. Here in the wilderness, a person would have to rely on whatever *they were given. Even more troubling, the Germans demanded the crops of the occupied country.*

Near the resistenza hideout, Francesco scampered up a rocky incline, his breathing steady as he hefted a bag of rice on his shoulder. Nico gasped for air as he lugged the other rice bag. He had never given much thought to physical exercise. Now, he regretted the hours spent painting in a chair.

"Need some help?" Francesco asked with an arched brow.

"No," Nico wheezed as he stopped to catch his breath. "I'm fine."

He gritted his teeth and forced himself to keep pace with Francesco's limber steps across the rock-strewn path. Francesco paused long enough to glance behind them, and Nico followed his gaze. The truck was still parked behind shrubbery, but the horizon remained clear, without any signs of a vehicle traveling on the dirt road. Light flakes drifted down to coat the mountains, but not enough to inhibit traffic.

With any luck, no one from the town would suddenly feel an urgent need to go to the mountains.

Nico followed Francesco into the dark cave. A fire still crackled in the center of the space, the warmth and flickering light a welcome respite from the harsh weather outside. A group of four men sat with hands outstretched over the fire, including Paolo. The other men of the resistance must be out on various missions. Francesco set the rice bag on the ground and handed the crumpled paper from the post office to Paolo.

Paolo unfolded the message. "You did well, Nico."

"He did," Francesco confirmed. "And you should know that the Nazis have finally entered our village. It appears they will make our town a reinforcement center, maybe another Winter Line to deter the Allies. In fact, one soldier followed us into the post office to see what Nico hung on the wall. Who knew Mussolini's face could prove so useful?" Francesco gave Nico a wry grin.

Paolo winced as he rose to his full height. "How many soldiers?"

"Too many to count." Francesco's voice quivered, suggesting the jovial farmer could feel fear after all.

"I suspect reinforcements are being pulled from Northern Italy and sent to Rome. How long before the Allies reach the city?" Paolo asked.

Nico cleared his throat. "They were approaching Monte Cassino, or so I've heard. Mind you, that was days ago. Anything could have changed since then."

"You've heard?" Paolo arched an eyebrow.

"I used to deliver propaganda posters to Captain Accardo in Rome. Snatches of conversation often drifted my way."

"What else did you learn?" Francesco asked. Nico felt the weight of every man's gaze on him, eyes glittering in the shadows. "Why were you privy to such information?"

His pulse skipped as he considered his words. Finally, he chose the truth. "I didn't just paint posters. I was called in to assess art. Most of it had been stolen from Jewish and Italian families."

Paolo's face hardened as his fists balled at his sides.

Nico met his gaze, resolved to take whatever came his way. "I never wanted to do either of those things for them. They threatened my nonna, and I thought I was keeping her safe. I didn't know how to escape it once I was in it. But now I want to make amends for the wrongs I've committed. That's the truth of it."

"You are here now. You can make a difference if you choose to."

Nico blinked furiously at the sudden wetness in his eyes. Of all the reactions possible from a resistance fighter, he had not expected mercy.

Francesco deftly changed the subject. "You can't stay here, Paolo. It's too close to town, and you could be discovered. But you and your men won't be able to leave easily. What will you do?"

Paolo tossed the note into the fire, watching the paper wither and curl into ash. "I need to send another message to coordinate our attacks. We'll have to join forces with the other resistenza bands, but to do so, I'll need someone to be my messenger. As you know, our radio broke, and I doubt I'll be able to find another. Our rations dip lower by the day, and this side of the mountain is likely to be exposed should the fight come to us."

"I'll carry your message," Nico said at once. "Where do you need me to go?"

Paolo seemed to accept his offer without question. "To Bologna. Use the painting again and pretend to sell it to a Fabio Venti as a Christmas present. Tell him that Paolo recommended you. He'll inspect it, but the frame sadly will appear loose. Give him a moment or two to find the message. He was a schoolteacher until recently, and he has a sharp eye. You'll find him on Capua Street. He'll have no choice but to refuse your painting, since you'll set the cost too high for something so damaged."

The directive sounded easy enough, even if he had no idea what resided in the messages.

Francesco folded his arms across his chest. "I can take Nico if need be. And I'll bring meat the next visit. I've tried to hold out at the farm as long as I can, leaving the animals for Nonna, but..."

The stable where Nico had found refuge? He couldn't imagine taking more from Francesco's grandmother and mother.

Paolo shook his head. "No, Francesco. Your family needs to eat."

"We'll keep a few cuts. You don't want to argue with the women in my family," Francesco said. "I will return for Nico tomorrow. For now, I need to go home and prepare my family for what may come." He turned to leave the cave, and Nico followed.

"Give my regards to them," Nico said.

"You are always welcome to return," Francesco replied. "The house remains open to those in need. Simply walk in."

"I think your mother would smack me if I tried something like that." Nico chuckled.

Francesco winked, but his expression sobered as he glanced over his shoulder to where the dirt road lay quiet, with a light covering of snow gathering at the edges.

Nico pulled his coat tight before returning to the cave. "I'll see you tomorrow?"

"God willing," Francesco said, his tone cryptic. He walked to his truck.

Nico realized Paolo and the others wanted to protect him, should the Nazis or Mussolini's soldiers detain him. But as he watched the departing truck move east, he wondered if Francesco did more for the resistance than run errands.

When Nico returned to the fire, he sank down on the cold ground and held his trembling hands over the flames. The other men watched him, old men with rugged beards and sullen youths with chapped cheeks dried from the bitter cold and wind.

He had never felt so afraid for Sophia. Yet he felt he could not let Paolo down.

One more task to help Paolo, and then I'll return to Rome.

Then he realized something. By now, Captain Accardo and Matteo would realize that Nico had fled the city, bringing suspicion of working with the resistance on him. It seemed likely that Sophia would be forced underground as well.

Shivering, he prayed again. So many miracles needed. Dare he continue to trust God to provide?

Paolo sat down again. "You are very quiet, Nico."

"I am always quiet," Nico responded with a small smile as he struggled to find a comfortable spot on the hard ground littered with rock and debris.

Paolo shuffled closer to him, keeping his voice low. "You can refuse, you know. I am putting you in danger as it stands. I won't lie to you. If you get caught passing messages, the sentence will be extreme."

An image of the rebellious Cubist painting confiscated by Captain Accardo flashed through Nico's mind.

He lifted his chin and met Paolo's eyes. "I've refused to deal with what's been in front of me for too many years. Truthfully, I'm more afraid of what I've become than of what they can do to me. I must take a stand. I have lost a bit of my soul every time I have compromised to suit those more powerful, those who seek to do injustice. What else do I have to lose? I have no family left. I have nothing, Paolo. I can only hope to earn my way back into the good graces of those I care about. Yet, I dare not think that any good I do now will be enough to redeem me after all I've done."

Paolo remained silent as he stretched his hands to the fire. The light of the flames cast an orange glow against his lean features. At last he said, "You cannot earn your salvation. None of us can. When you painted the Nativity, what thoughts came to your mind?"

"I wanted to feel hope. To focus on what my nonna taught me as a boy. I was homesick, thinking of yet another Christmas spent alone. I wanted to believe in miracles again."

"Our Savior's story is the greatest miracle. Our Messiah, born of a virgin, came to save us and give us the gift of Himself, taking our sins in an act of sacrifice. He gives us His righteousness, and we belong to Him. Not to Captain Accardo or the secret police, or the party, or anything else that demands our allegiance. We belong to Him. It is up to you whether you receive God's gift of forgiveness. He will not force it on you. But believe me, you will never wash away the stains inside you on your own. You cannot earn your way to heaven. We need Him to make the way for us."

Paolo's impassioned words sank into Nico as they sat by the flickering fire. Could he find forgiveness and, after that, peace again? The very idea felt foreign and remote to him.

"Do you have the painting?" Paolo asked, breaking the lull in the conversation.

Nico got up and retrieved the leather satchel, where the painting lay safe. He pulled it out and pried apart the frame as carefully as he could, revealing the hollow chamber.

Paolo turned away from Nico, scribbling on a scrap of paper. He shifted slightly, revealing a glimpse of a few numbers. Perhaps coordinates for a location.

Paolo slid the paper into the hollow. The frame felt loose in Nico's hands as he fit it together once more. But he didn't have any nails to secure it. How many more trips could it make before everything fell apart?

Mary's clear-eyed gaze followed Nico as he pressed the frame together again.

Somehow, he felt the same as the wobbly frame. As if one slight move might jar everything loose within him.

CHAPTER TWENTY-TWO

*D*ebbie pushed open the door to the café. No singing greeted her this Wednesday morning, no music from the speakers. But the sound of pots banging alerted her to Janet's presence.

"Is Ian feeling any better?" Debbie asked as she hung up her coat and purse in the kitchen.

Janet glanced over her shoulder as she placed raw scones on the baking sheet. They were loaded with plump raisins and plenty of cinnamon. "Hey there. Yes, he's going to survive. I wasn't too thrilled with him traipsing about the countryside when it's so cold out. But he slept well last night and seems to be on the mend this morning. I, on the other hand, didn't sleep much at all."

Before Debbie could reply, a voice calling from the café drew her out of the kitchen.

Tim Croft strode up to the counter. "Have you seen Kim? I wanted to chat with her."

Debbie paused. "Not yet. I'm sure she'll arrive soon. Is something wrong?"

He brushed snow from his tousled hair. "One of the sheep got hurt at the Nativity. I'm not too happy about it. If we do the live Nativity next year, we'll need to make some changes with the security."

"I'm sorry to hear about your sheep. Greg told me that the rope securing the pens was loosened."

He gestured to the art wall. "Yeah. And I heard that someone stole the painting in the café, likely around the same time."

"Did you see anything unusual?"

He rubbed his chin. "I saw that guy in the beige coat going back and forth in front of the animal pens with his camera. The other cameraman was filming the station and the track. I asked the guy in the beige coat why he didn't go on the train, but he said that he was supposed to film the train entering the station."

Victor in his beige coat, who silently followed Jude and Maurice with his camera. Could he be responsible for the theft?

"You didn't see anyone carrying a painting or notice anything else that seemed strange?" she asked.

"I'm not under investigation, am I? No, I didn't see anyone leaving the café. I was too busy trying to get ahold of my son on the train." Tim pulled out his phone and showed Debbie his text thread with Brad. "See the time of the messages? Then I had a donkey to chase. I think you need to chat with the cameraman in the beige coat."

Debbie sensed a movement to her right. Janet stepped up beside her.

Tim stuck his phone into his pocket. "Good day, ladies." He turned on his heel and left the café.

"He seems pretty upset," Janet commented.

"I agree, but I don't think he's responsible for the theft." Debbie shared what she and Greg had discussed the night before.

Janet folded her arms across her chest. "I had wondered about Brad's involvement in the theft based on his gossip about Ricky. It's like he wants to ruin Ricky's reputation. But I agree—I don't think he or his father stole the painting. I'm leaning more toward Leo or Maurice. What do you think?"

"Tim mentioned the cameraman in the beige coat. You know, I saw a beige coat outside the café the night someone rattled the kitchen door. But Tim and Victor both have beige coats."

"Should we talk to Victor?" Janet asked. "I'll definitely let Ian know about your conversation with Tim just now too."

Debbie nodded. "We also need to talk to Paulette again. And perhaps we should do a reverse image search of the painting online and see if it makes it onto some resale site."

"That's a great idea. But we'll have to move fast. Christmas isn't too far away, and I'd rather find answers sooner than later."

"Me too. For Ricky's sake and that of the station. Poor Kim. She must be so overwhelmed right now. She put so much work into that event only to have it sabotaged by someone who wanted to use it for their own selfish ends."

The bell above the café door tinkled, and Ricky entered, stamping his boots on the mat.

"The very man we wanted to see," Debbie said.

"Hi, Debbie." Ricky shoved a hand through his hair until the ends stood up. "Can we talk?"

"Let me bring coffee," she said as she grabbed the pot from the coffee machine. She looped her fingers through the handles of two mugs with the other hand, brought everything to a table, and poured the coffee. "Can I get you anything to eat?"

He shook his head, his expression miserable. "I have no appetite. And I cook for a living. I love food. This past week, I've been so uptight that I've lost my appetite for everything I normally enjoy."

She put the coffeepot back on the heater and took a seat at Ricky's table. "Janet and I were discussing the missing painting. I want you to know how sorry I am that it disappeared on our watch. We all feel terrible, so I can't imagine how sad you must feel. Especially when your family treasured the Nativity piece for so long."

He met her gaze. "I want you to know that I don't blame you for what happened. Or Janet. Or Paulette. Or Kim. You all are my friends and like family to my wife and me. I know you never would have let something like this happen out of negligence."

"I'll do everything I can to find it. We're going to try a reverse search online, using a photograph of the painting. That way, if anyone tries to sell it there, we'll be able to find out. Ian came by to check the video feed from the camera. We found nothing."

"Nothing?" Ricky frowned. "What did the camera show?"

"Crosby appeared agitated, and as Paulette noted, the café had no traffic. The feed showed no one coming into the café at all."

He shook his head. "I don't get it. It's almost as if someone cut the power to the camera."

A chill rippled through her at the idea. "No, the video kept running. No power outages were reported at the station or café."

"Do you think more than one person was involved in the theft?"

"That's a possibility. We wondered if Leo might be involved, especially considering his reaction to you when he discovered the painting on the wall?"

"Leo's always resented me. We've never gotten along well. He hated the restaurant, claiming he would never stand for being trapped in a hot, greasy kitchen even if our grandfather loved it. I, however, loved learning to cook at my grandfather's side. My best memories happened in that kitchen. Why shouldn't Grandfather leave the restaurant to me? I spent every summer I had with him while Leo gallivanted about Ohio, determined to live life his way. Now he resents me for the relationship I had with our grandfather, but I put in the effort. Leo had the right to lead his own life, but he has no right to complain about the natural results of his choices."

Debbie swallowed. Clearly, her question had poked a deep wound. "Would he ever try to take the painting from you?"

"He did years ago." Ricky's mouth flattened into a thin line. "After Grandfather died, Leo loaded the painting into the car. I stopped him at the last second and pulled it from his trunk. In the end, the lawyer of the estate had to show Leo the will to prove Grandfather had left it to me. That was a day to remember. Two Carosi men, as hotheaded as could be, telling each other how things would go."

"Oh, Ricky. I'm sorry things got so bad between you two."

"I'm not proud of that moment, Debbie. I said terrible things, things I can't take back, even if I felt justified when I said them."

"Did you ever apologize to him?"

Ricky nudged aside the coffee cup. "Why bother? What if he really did take the painting this time? No, I'm not the one who needs to apologize. He is. He insulted me, accusing me of turning Grandfather against him. I would never do that. But I did tell Leo that he was selfish for abandoning Grandfather for so long."

"I hear you. If you don't mind me asking, what's your story with Brad?"

Ricky grimaced. "I didn't want to make a big deal about that. I tried to protect his pride, but he often came in late and left early. He was always searching for the easy way out. He had grandiose ideas about running a fancy restaurant. This is Dennison, Ohio, not New York. And he wasn't reliable with the duties he was given. You don't cut corners in a kitchen. You want to be frugal and efficient, but you never cheat the customer. The last straw was the time he served a chocolate lava cake without my special raspberry sauce. I had asked him to make the sauce an hour prior. He didn't, and I gave him a piece of my mind. You must have noticed the tension between him and me."

"I also overheard him complaining about the situation. He felt he had been treated unfairly."

Ricky scowled. "Not at all. I gave him more chances than I should have and offered to mentor him in his spare time. Finally, I had to fire him. Is he working in the restaurant business now?"

"No, I think he's still on the farm, helping his dad. I heard he has plans to go to culinary school."

"Oh? He's in for a rough spell there. Some of those chefs run their kitchens like a Marine boot camp."

"Maybe he'll grow up and learn."

Ricky rose from the table, his expression grim. "I sure hope so. I want Brad to be happy, but he sure does get in his own way."

The day rolled by as Debbie served customers. Paulette operated the cash register while Janet stayed busy in the kitchen. A steady stream of visitors came to the café, purchasing, consoling, asking questions, and clucking their tongues when Debbie or Paulette recounted the stories.

If Debbie never fielded another question about trains again, it would be too soon.

The one person who didn't waltz through the café doors was Maurice Devons.

Jude wandered in for a mocha around lunchtime and ordered a cappuccino with extra cinnamon. Victor came in with him, silent as always, and with the glum countenance he had worn since she had first met him. Did the man ever smile?

"How are you today?" Jude asked as he pulled out his wallet to pay. He wore a rust-hued tweed jacket with suede patches at the elbow. The cream scarf looped around his neck gave him an extra snazzy appearance. If Maurice appeared the rhinestone cowboy, Jude seemed determined to channel the polished English gentleman.

"Busy, at least," Debbie overheard Paulette say.

"That's good. I heard about the painting as well. I'm so sorry about the loss and the damage to the train. Any news regarding what happened?"

Debbie hurried to set her empty tray in the kitchen, eager to hear more of the conversation. As she headed back to the counter, Paulette said, "It's as if the painting disappeared into thin air."

Jude frowned. "My fellow cameramen and I noticed a few families outside the café. There was also the farmer, the one with the animals. What was his name?"

"Tim Croft. His son, Brad, played a role in the Nativity," Paulette answered as she slid the white cup topped with foam over to him.

"How long will you be staying in town?" Debbie cut in.

Jude glanced at her. "Not long. Maurice intends to leave soon. He's ordered us to get our final shots of the town and surrounding countryside today and pack up a day or two ahead of schedule. It'll be intense, but worth it. I haven't had a Christmas with family in a long while. That's the price you pay when you seek fame. The working hours are atrocious."

Should she be concerned about Maurice's apparent schedule? She needed to talk with him again, preferably with Janet or Ian by her side. "Someone mentioned seeing Victor by the animals. Do you think Victor might be able to shed some light on how the animals were let loose?"

"Let's see." Jude waved for Victor to come forward to the counter. "Debbie has questions for you."

Victor frowned as he approached. "About what?"

"Did you see anyone try to enter the café or release the animals from the pen?"

"Nothing unusual. We caught quite a bit of the events on film, though."

"Maybe you can share that footage with our police chief and his deputies?" Debbie pressed. "I bet they wouldn't mind reviewing it. Perhaps you caught something crucial that will help them crack the case."

"That's a great idea," Jude said. "We'd be glad to send the police chief whatever we can."

She grabbed a pen and paper to get Jude's phone number. "I'll have them call you."

"Speaking of cracking cases…," Jude muttered under his breath. He tipped his head toward the entrance. "That's the man you need to talk to—the train engineer who caused the derailment."

Leo Carosi came in, twisting his cap in his hands.

"It's been nice chatting with you. I'm relieved everyone is doing well considering the train accident. I'll stop by before we head out of town and take a box of doughnuts for the road." Jude reached for his cappuccino before moving out of the way at the counter, but he didn't go far.

"I appreciate your help," Debbie said. She gave Leo a welcoming smile.

Leo took the cue and approached the glass counter. "Do you have a moment to chat?"

She checked the clock. "I think I have a few minutes."

"Go," Paulette said to Debbie. "I'll take care of anyone who comes in." She was wonderfully intuitive whenever Debbie needed to dig into an investigation.

Debbie led Leo to an empty table. Jude lingered a moment longer, his gaze snagging on hers before he finally headed out the door.

"I'm here for a couple of reasons," Leo began haltingly as he set his cap on the table. It was a train conductor's hat with thin white and blue stripes. "I'm not blind to the gossip roaring through town. I heard snippets of conversation at the grocery store. I'm getting all kinds of stares. I did not cause that train accident, Debbie."

"I should think Kim will have answers soon enough with what caused the train mishap. Have you talked further with her?"

"Yes. Ian spoke with me as well. I understand that someone might have fiddled with the railway switch."

She frowned. "Last I heard, that was merely a suspicion, a theory."

"It's been confirmed."

She made a mental note to call Ian as soon as she could.

"And the painting?" she began delicately as she leaned forward.

He blanched. "Don't tell me I'm a suspect in that too. I would never take it. Even if it belongs to me, I've never demanded it. Of course I was shocked when I heard the results of my grandfather's will. He knew how much I loved the Nativity scene. How much I wanted to learn more about Nico. Every time I asked Grandfather about Nico, he would shrug and say Nico wanted nothing to do with him. That answer never sat right with me. Why would Nico send the painting to someone he wanted nothing to do with?"

"I'm trying to find out more about Nico too. Would it be possible for you and Ricky to talk to each other? Maybe come to some kind of understanding before Christmas?"

Leo's eyes watered, but he pushed away from the table all the same, indicating the conversation was over. "I wish I could, Debbie, but Ricky wrote me off long ago. No, I don't think we can talk."

He left her at the table as she mulled over his words. One thing struck her. Either Leo had forgotten that he had tried to take the painting from Ricky years before, or one of the cousins had deliberately lied to her about it.

CHAPTER TWENTY-THREE

Outside Brisighella, Italy
December 24, 1943

The past several weeks had been a blur. Today was no exception as Nico retrieved several notes within the painting's frame, courtesy of a sympathetic antiques dealer who sent money to the resistenza. Despite the dim light of the cave, he carefully tucked in the canvas and gently tapped the frame snugly against the painting, reflecting that he could probably do this with his eyes closed. He had stretched the canvas over and over with each trip. And he had saved the miniature nails, inserting them into different spots to maintain the integrity of the wood.

He had traveled at dawn and at night, all across the countryside, heading into villages and lonely farmsteads. People greeted him with suspicion until they heard he came on behalf of Paolo. The Nativity painting with the infant Jesus eased fears too. Then, when Nico pried open the frame, revealing the slips of paper—which he never read, per Paolo's instructions—faces shone with renewed hope.

"You are an angel of mercy," one middle-aged woman told him as she clutched her young daughter. The little girl gazed up at him with large brown eyes, her hair gathered into twin braids. The small family stood in the doorway of a decrepit apartment, the mother glancing nervously left and right down the narrow street. "You've brought us good news. We were desperate until you came."

"I'm no angel," he said wryly as he slid the painting back into the stained satchel. He was more a sinner than a saint. But now, he felt strangely light. Instead of keeping silent amid the theft of artwork and creating propaganda, he used his art to do something better. Something that mattered.

If only he knew what it was that brought the light to the men and women he found. But he would never betray Paolo's confidence by reading the slips himself, no matter how tempting.

When he had left the woman in the doorway, he overheard her murmur to her child, "Go get your bag, mia cara. We leave now. It's safe. I promise. We have a place to hide."

In the shadows of the cave, he paused over the painting, his vision bleary from the lack of sleep. Would he run into more of the gaunt but hardened resistenza fighters hidden in nearby farms today? Or would he deliver a secret message to another trembling family? He could never tell who he would encounter. He simply did as Paolo and Francesco bid him. He wondered if some of the messages contained locations of safe houses for those hunted by the Nazis. Others' messages might carry secret intel for the scattered pockets of fighters stationed in the mountains and nearby villages.

Meanwhile, the world outside the cave grew colder. The land seemed more dangerous and fierce with the sounds of shelling rumbling in the distance. Paolo and his men left on daring missions, often gone for hours. Some did not return.

When Nico had begged to fight with him, Paolo had refused.

"No. You are needed as messenger. I have no one else who can do this. Please. For my sake and Sophia's."

Thoughts of returning to Rome had nearly vanished, yet Nico still longed to find Sophia. But as the weeks passed, he feared he might not be able to ride the train. Rumors swept through of the Allies pressing ever closer to Rome. Hitler proved a vicious man when cornered. Mussolini as well. The noose tightened, but still the occupying country refused to release its vise-like grip.

Nico sank down in the cave and grabbed a blanket, determined to nap until Paolo's return. He awoke to voices, including Paolo's. The men clamored with barely concealed excitement. Then he heard a woman's voice filter through the cacophony, low and sweet.

For a moment, he thought he dreamed. How else could he hear that particular voice? Then the men parted and there she stood in the cave, with Paolo's arm around her shoulders. Her once-glorious hair was shorn like a man's. Trousers and a shapeless coat hid her willowy frame. Yet he would recognize her eyes anywhere.

She had never appeared more beautiful to him.

"Look who we found half a mile outside of the caves," Francesco announced.

Nico stood, his throat tightening until he couldn't force any words through it. How had she escaped Rome?

Her gaze snagged on his, and for one moment, he saw fear, exultation...and something else he couldn't quite define. "Nico. You made it to the mountains."

He finally found his voice. "H-how did you escape?"

"I left the day after you did. Your neighbor, Mia Ginerva, kept me hidden in her apartment as long as she could. Your flat was ransacked shortly after you left, and I knew I had to go too. If I had remained there, I shudder to think what might have happened. I could not go home. The situation grew worse when Mia went to the bakery to see if she could speak to my father. She found out that he had been ordered to give up my whereabouts, but he couldn't because he didn't know them. There was nothing I could do but leave the city. Mia suggested I cut my hair and dress like a boy and find rides with anyone willing to help a stranger in need."

"It's a miracle," Paolo murmured as he drew his sister to his side. "I cannot tell you how grateful I am to see you again, safe and sound."

A miracle indeed. Nico had experienced many during the past several weeks. More than enough to trust that God truly saw him and others. Hope wasn't lost after all.

Sophia's eyes gleamed as she hugged her brother. "You say that now, but I fear I've been followed. I think I lost some SS soldiers several miles back, but I can't be certain."

The men's faces paled at her words. A few even dashed out to join the two men stationed as watchers. Fortunately, when they returned, they declared the road winding through the mountains to be clear. The tension that had built in the cave eased.

In Nico's spare moments, he had tried to plan what he would say to Sophia if and when he should see her again. But now that she stood before him, he couldn't remember anything he'd come up with.

Paolo sat by the fire. To Nico's surprise, Sophia sank down beside him rather than her brother.

When he recovered from his shock, he whispered to her, "Please tell me my neighbor will be safe."

"Yes, but you won't find Mia again if you return to Rome. I found her a haven—at least until the Allies come and liberate the city."

He shoved a hand through his hair, relieved but curious as to how Sophia had hidden the old woman. "Where are the Allies now?"

"Held up at Monte Cassino with fierce fighting. Mussolini and Hitler intend to dig in until the bitter end. We must pray the Allies make it before more good people find themselves endangered."

"You passed the checkpoints all right?" He immediately chided himself. Obviously she had, as she sat beside him.

She gave him a patient smile. "As a boy, yes. Matteo put out a search for me. My face is plastered all over Rome as Sophia Giudice. I miss my long hair, but this short style is infinitely easier to manage. Actually, I would have been forced to join the army if not for a kind farmer and his wife who pretended I was their young son. They drove me part of the way here, past the checkpoints. I hitchhiked or walked the rest of the way."

His stomach rolled at the mention of Matteo and the idea of Sophia's lovely face plastered on wanted posters throughout the city. Plenty of brave women had enlisted in the resistenza, but how many of them had earned a poster all their own? He wanted to ask more about her role in the resistenza and the secret hideaways she knew about in the city, but a strangled shout echoed from outside the cave.

"Put out the fire!" Paolo cried as he leaped to his feet, scattering pebbles.

In a blur, the men followed his lead, snatching their rifles and bags. One of them grabbed a nearby pail loaded with dirt and dumped it out over the flames, smothering them.

Pulse pounding, Nico dove for his painting and his satchel. No longer did he carry propaganda posters. During his stay, he had used every single one of them in attempts to deflect attention.

He had just slung the strap of his satchel over his shoulder when the fire's light went out in the cave. Someone switched on a flashlight, the bulb flickering and weak, but it was enough for him to search the cave for Sophia. Chaos reigned as the men dashed out into the cold. Twilight fell, coating the mountainside in hues of purple. In the distance, where the road ran through the mountains, Nico spotted lights, to his horror. Several, in fact, suggesting a convoy of considerable size.

"We've been found," Francesco said, his tone matter-of-fact as he shouldered past Nico. He tugged a cap over his wild curls, and Nico realized that the young man had a rifle slung over his shoulder.

"Is it the Germans?"

"Probably," Paolo said. "Whoever it is, we cannot stay here." He grasped Nico's arm. "I must beg you to do one last thing for me. Something of the greatest importance. I shall forever be in your debt for it."

"Anything," Nico answered without hesitation.

"I need you to take my sister to the Allies. We have one last message, if you can protect her. Please get her out of here. Run far and fast. Don't look behind you. Don't let her stop. You're the one person I trust to do this, Nico."

"I'll do it." He felt foolish and inadequate even as he agreed. Fear rose within him. "Will you write the message down?"

"Ask Sophia after you are both clear of danger. She'll tell you what to do." Then Paolo hugged him tightly. "Go with God. May He keep both of you safe, Nico."

A band of brothers. Nico's eyes filled, but the lights drew closer, and the audible rumble of vehicles echoed in the mountains. He rushed to Sophia, seizing her hand without a second thought. "I'm sorry to pull you away from your family, but your brother asked me to escort you out of the mountains."

"Paolo!" she cried.

Her brother paused, then dashed to engulf her in a tight embrace—perhaps the siblings' last. "Don't cry, little sister. And do not blame yourself. Give me this one gift, to know that you will survive no matter what happens. Never forget how loved you are. Nico has promised to take care of you. You can trust him."

"Paolo, I don't want to leave you."

He took her fair cheeks in his large, chapped hands. "You won't, ever. We will always have family, mia cara, no matter where the wind takes us. Nico is proof of that. He has been as a brother to me since he came here for you."

She took Nico's hand in a tight grip.

Francesco, who had waited for Paolo, waved at them. "My grandmother will welcome you if need be. If you see her, tell her Francesco stayed in the mountains for another round of adventures."

Nico wanted to answer with something as cheerful and carefree as Francesco, but shots resounded, the sound cracking in the cold air. The men hurried to take their positions as Nico tugged Sophia close.

Together, they ran into the night as darkness fell.

CHAPTER TWENTY-FOUR

*L*ate Wednesday afternoon, Debbie helped Janet close the cash register at the café, then checked her phone. Her weather app predicted seven inches of snow from a snowstorm that threatened to overtake Dennison and the surrounding area by early evening.

In an earlier phone call, Ian had informed her that he couldn't share too many details regarding the switch being tampered with as Leo had claimed. That was understandable, considering Ian's professional role.

"Did Jude get in touch with you?" she'd asked him, hoping to learn about the investigation into the painting theft as well.

"He did," Ian replied, his voice still hoarse. "I had a chance to review their footage. They seemed to aim their cameras everywhere but the front of the café and the station. I guess the parking lot held all the action. Tim was in all the footage, whether on his phone or running after the animals. I saw Jude try to help round up sheep. It looks like Victor filmed much of it."

"Tim couldn't be an accomplice," she mused. "And his son, Brad, was with us for the play. I think we can rule both of them out on the theft. I wondered about Victor, but if he was busy filming, then I'm not sure who snuck into the café."

"I agree," Ian said. "We'll keep searching, Debbie. For now, I have to go."

He hadn't sent any updates since that conversation. She was about to put her phone back in her purse when a message came through that lightened her heart. Greg asked if she wanted to watch *It's a Wonderful Life* with the boys.

She texted an enthusiastic, Yes! I'll make a candy run beforehand.

Can you get popcorn? I think I used the last of my supply for the tree, Greg typed back. Julian has politely requested red licorice. He promises to share with his brother this time.

Debbie chuckled as she typed back her agreement.

"That smile of yours brightens my day," Janet said as she removed her apron.

"I'm off to watch a Christmas movie with Greg and the boys. Honestly, I can't wait to put my feet up and take my mind off everything."

Janet flicked off the lights in the kitchen. "I'm glad Jaxon has finally warmed up to you."

"It's taken a while, but it's well worth the wait. And I do have a secret weapon."

"Oh?"

"Yes, I'm off to do a candy run. Julian's promising to share his favorite kind with Jaxon this time."

Janet laughed as she shrugged into her coat. "Those boys. They may not always get along, but they care about each other."

"They're good kids," Debbie said. "I've so enjoyed getting to know them better."

"You should." Janet gave her a wink. "Who knows what the future will hold?"

"Let's not get ahead of ourselves by moving too fast." As soon as the warning left Debbie, she immediately wanted to take the words back. She and Greg hadn't moved fast. Instead, he had pursued a relationship with her at a healthy pace, ever respectful and considerate. If anything, she was ready for more commitment.

Janet hummed under her breath as she buttoned her coat. "You never know. Things could change mighty quickly. Regardless, they're good boys."

Debbie grinned in return as she grabbed her parka. Yes, Julian and Jaxon were close. Brothers ought to be considered a gift.

"I think you and I should talk to Leo and Maurice tomorrow. We need to nail the theft of the painting down to something concrete," Debbie suggested.

"Maybe Paulette can close for us so we can leave early. I suspect the crowds will thin out now that Maurice plans on leaving." Janet slid on her mittens.

Debbie's phone dinged again, this time with a text from Kim. I'VE HEARD BACK FROM THE FEDERAL RAILROAD ADMINISTRATION. THEY SENT FIELD PERSONNEL TO ASSESS THE ACCIDENT. THEY BELIEVE THE TRAIN DIDN'T SPEED, BUT IT DID GO TOO FAST TO MAKE THE SWITCH. THEY CONCLUDED THAT SOMEONE PULLED THE SWITCH DELIBERATELY. THE INVESTIGATION IS HEATING UP, DEBBIE. I CAN'T SAY MUCH MORE, BUT DO TELL JANET TO STAY SAFE. I KNOW YOU BOTH ARE ON THE CASE, BUT I DON'T WANT EITHER OF YOU GETTING HURT. THIS IS ONE FOR THE PROFESSIONALS, OKAY?

"You stopped smiling," Janet observed as she adjusted her scarf. "Is something wrong?"

Too shocked to speak, Debbie handed the phone to her friend.

Janet gasped. "Why would someone do such a thing to a train full of families?"

"And we have the missing painting to boot."

"Could the two be connected somehow?"

Debbie considered the question. "I don't know, but the stakes keep rising. I think we have to consider that option."

"Since Leo and Maurice were on the train, can we assume they didn't have anything to do with the stolen painting?" Janet asked.

"I don't think we can assume that at this point. What if Leo or Maurice arranged for the painting to be taken by someone else? Leo thought the artwork rightfully belonged to him. Maurice had the audacity to take the painting off the wall the first time he saw it. I doubt he'd shy away from doing it again, or ordering someone else to."

Janet nodded thoughtfully. "What about the Crofts?"

"I don't think it could be Brad or Tim. Tim was too preoccupied rounding up the sheep. Victor filmed the animals escaping and Tim chasing them with Jude's help, and Brad was on the train with us."

Janet folded her arms over her chest. "I appreciate Jude being so helpful. We really are stepping into something dangerous if someone was willing to derail a train full of people over this. I just wish I knew who."

"Me too. I think we should meet with Maurice tomorrow morning before he leaves town."

"Let me talk to Ian first. We may need Deputy Vaughn's help, especially with Ian under the weather. I know Ian won't discuss the particulars of cases with me—professional duty and all—but I have a feeling Kim's already sent me the same text that she sent you. She's sending us a warning to slow down."

"I hate slowing down," Debbie said. "And I promised Ricky I would investigate the theft. I'll leave the train investigation to the professionals, but if the crimes aren't connected, there's no harm in my asking questions to find a stolen family heirloom painting, is there?"

"And if they are connected?"

Debbie met her friend's gaze. "Then the sooner we find the perpetrator, the better for all of us. We'll get there faster by investigating on multiple fronts, and you know it as well as I do."

"I was afraid you'd say that." Janet massaged her temples. "This could get interesting."

Later that evening, Debbie parked in front of the grocery store and hurried inside to get the red licorice and popcorn for the boys and Greg. Funny how she had started to think of Jaxon and Julian as "the boys," rather than "Greg's boys." Almost as if they were *her* boys. She paid the cashier and grabbed the paper bag loaded with candy, popcorn, and a few diet sodas.

As she exited the glass door, a man nearly bumped into her.

"Jude?" she cried out, trying not to slip on the ice.

"Debbie!" He caught her arms and helped her regain her footing. "It's freezing. What are you doing out on a night like this?"

"Getting movie treats," she said with a grin, even though she felt a tinge of wariness after Kim's last message.

"A worthy cause, I'm sure. This weather makes me long for Miami. It's seventy-six degrees by the beach right now, Debbie. Don't tell me that doesn't sound fabulous."

"Not to me. I adore the snow," Debbie answered.

"I'll get to the beach for both of us soon enough. I'm flying out to see my girlfriend for Christmas. She's been begging me to spend a holiday with her and her family," he said with a wink.

"I'm glad you get a holiday."

"It'll be the first of many," he told her. "I've decided I'm going to quit the show. I can't take the pressure anymore, I'm tired of missing people I care about, and Maurice is impossible." Jude shoved his gloved hands into his coat pockets.

"What's going on with Maurice?"

"He's frustrated with the winter storm headed our way. I guess the forecaster said the roads leading out of Dennison might be closed until the plows can get to them. So he might not be able to leave as early as he hopes to. He's also obsessed with that painting of the Nativity. It's what a lot of antique dealers do—they all want to buy low and sell high. It's how they make a profit. But I'm tired of working for the 'Cowboy Collector.' Between you and me, he's actually from Atlanta. He's never wrangled a cow or a horse in his life. The cowboy bit is an act for the ladies."

"I'm speechless," Debbie said as she held her bag of groceries, her fingers numb from the cold. She wasn't all that surprised, but she wanted to keep him talking.

Jude offered her an apologetic shrug. "Showbiz tends to be ruthless. I'm thinking of working freelance. Maybe get a contracting job in Miami with a local news station. Do some serious work on something other than antiques for once."

"I wish you the best of luck on your new venture, Jude. Have a wonderful Christmas."

"I will, but say a little prayer for me when I tell Maurice. I'm dreading it already." Jude shivered. "Hope I survive the famous Maurice Devons wrath. His behavior toward his staff is always atrocious. That's one reason I can't work with him any longer. Whatever fame I might ride his coattails to isn't worth the abuse."

She felt that she might be treading on thin ice. "Do you think Maurice might know more about the painting than we realize? He's got motive to take it, given how much he wanted it."

Jude raised an eyebrow. "I know I'm not putting him in a flattering light, but how could Maurice have taken the painting if he was on the train when it was stolen? Are you sure it wasn't Leo? Remember how angry Leo was when he realized his precious painting hung on the café wall? And what if that farmer, Tim and his son, planned the whole thing? They could have worked together to cause the distraction both at the café and on the railroad tracks. No, I think your attention is better spent elsewhere. If I see or hear anything of interest, I'll call you or Kim. Sorry, I can't stay and chat. I have to get supper for the crew. I'm hoping this grocery store carries fried chicken in the deli area."

"They do," she said. "Have a merry Christmas if I don't see you again."

He waved at her, his smile bright once more as he disappeared into the grocery store.

The second he was gone, she bent down to study the ground where he'd stood. His shoe print didn't have the distinctive treads Ian had shown her. She blew out a frosty breath. Jude seemed very certain about the identity of the thieves. Had she missed something in her questioning?

Her phone rang. She flinched at the time as she answered it.

"Are you okay?" came Greg's concerned voice through the speaker. "The weather is getting rough."

"I'm fine. I got sidetracked. Sorry to worry you."

"Let me guess. The painting?"

"Yes, I ran into Jude. He hinted that Leo might be responsible. But I'm not so sure." Debbie glanced over her shoulder at the grocery store as she hurried across the parking lot to her car. "And I'd like to know how he is."

It's a Wonderful Life played in the background. Julian and Jaxon munched on candy and handfuls of popcorn. It was the ideal winter's night, with fat flakes of snow swirling down past the windows.

However, Debbie and Greg stood in the kitchen, talking in hushed tones. She had run an internet search on the Nativity painting to see if it might appear on a website. So far, nothing. Did the thief have a private buyer lined up instead?

"Who do you think stole the painting?" Greg asked quietly.

She closed her eyes against the headache beginning to form. She'd been over this again and again, to no avail. "Maurice certainly has the money to bribe someone. Leo swears the train accident was simply that—an accident. Or maybe it was one of the camera crew under orders from Maurice. I just keep going around in circles about it."

"Right. We don't have enough information yet," Greg replied. "Do you have a next step?"

At least Debbie could answer that. "I'm going to talk to Maurice tomorrow morning. Jude hinted that he wants to leave early, but our Ohio winter weather should keep him here for a while. I saw Jude's footprint tonight at the grocery store. It doesn't match Ian's photo. Of course, most of us own more than one pair of boots or shoes. But I can't shake the notion that whoever caused the train wreck had someone else steal the painting. They must be connected somehow."

Greg took her hand. "I'll go with you. Plus, we ought to include Ian if we're going to chat with one of his suspects."

She liked the idea of the two of them working together. She also liked their quiet companionship, holding Greg's hand in his kitchen against the backdrop of a familiar old movie and the boys' laughter. Somehow, even in the midst of all the chaos, it felt as if she had come home.

"You know," she said wistfully, "when I hear Julian and Jaxon enjoying *It's A Wonderful Life,* it reminds me of my childhood. I always wanted to share those beautiful moments with kids of my own. But then I never had kids." Her hand slipped from Greg's grip. Was she being presumptuous to admit that she wanted to share more of her life with Greg's sons?

He put her fear to rest at once. "Debbie, they care about you. The boys and I talked a lot after the train accident. You've become so much a part of our lives. Not just mine, but theirs too. They never want to see you hurt, and they both admitted to me that you were the first person they thought of after they checked on me and each other." Greg swallowed. He took her hand again, intertwining their fingers. "You said you couldn't imagine your life without me."

"It's true," she told him, searching his face. "Jaxon and Julian are starting to feel like my boys. I worry about them, even if I'm not their mom. I enjoy being with them. In fact, I never want times like this evening to end."

He reached for her, cupping her cheek with his calloused palm. "Debbie, there's something I have to tell you. It's been on my mind for so long, and I—"

"Hey, are you guys going to watch the movie or what?" Julian called from the living room. "All the candy will be gone in the next sixty seconds if you don't join us."

She chuckled weakly, the moment shattered.

Greg dropped her hand with a sigh. "Coming," he called out, although he didn't sound all that enthused.

She couldn't blame him. What exactly had he wanted to say to her? Her heart pounded in an unsteady rhythm as she tried to regain a sense of normalcy following such an exchange.

Greg grabbed a bag of chips from the kitchen counter, but when he glanced at her, something flashed in his eyes. Something she could easily interpret as regret. But regret over what?

And as she glanced outside the window, where the harsh winter storm moaned against the glass panes, she knew she couldn't wait much longer to get her answers. From Maurice or from Greg.

CHAPTER TWENTY-FIVE

Faenza, Italy
December 24, 1943

Snowflakes swirled about Nico as he tucked Sophia close to his chest. A bitter wind blew across the dark countryside, obscuring their footprints while numbing his face, fingers, and toes. He glanced down at her bowed head. Her steps faltered as she leaned into him, trembling.

They had fled into the night without stopping, taking a route northeast, far from Francesco's sweet grandmother.

An ache settled in Nico's chest when he considered the sacrifice of the men in the mountains. Paolo had created enough of a distraction to give them an escape. And though Nico carried out Paolo's wishes, sorrow filled him. Would he see Paolo again? Or Francesco, who fed the *resistenza* and took care of everyone?

During the flight, Sophia had said nothing, her face pale. Surely she worried as Nico did.

At last she broke her silence. "How much farther, do you think?" Her voice barely reached him over the howling wind.

"I don't know," he admitted as he tightened his arm around her waist, all but carrying her across the frozen ground. "Just a few more steps across the hill, and then we'll see. Stay with me, Sophia."

"Just a few more steps," she echoed wearily.

He adjusted the angle of his body, providing what shelter he could from the intense wind. "If I have to carry you, I will."

"No need," she said, her face burrowed in his chest. She had escaped Rome, fleeing on foot with hardly any food. The shock of possibly losing her brother had likely stolen the last of her strength. "Once I catch my breath, I'll be fine."

How long had they already walked? He had lost track, the fear of capture driving him without mercy. A prayer whispered through him. In spite of her words, he bent and swept her off her feet, one arm around her back, the other tucked in the crook of her knees.

"No, Nico," she protested. "You must save your strength."

"Don't worry about me." She hardly weighed anything, due to those wretched rations. He trudged up the steep hill, his noisy breaths mingling with the crunch of his boots on the snow and brittle grass. "It's just for a bit," he said. "We can't stop. The Nazis have trucks, and we only have our feet."

He was not an athletic man like Matteo, but somehow he made it to the top of the hill. A magnificent sight stretched in front of him. Sophia stirred in his arms to see it as well. Through a break in the clouds, a glittering sky waited, diamonds studding an expanse of obsidian. Beneath it, rolling hills were dusted with white, now gleaming beneath the muted light of the moon.

Sophia groaned. "More hills to walk."

Without even thinking, he pressed a kiss to the top of her head. He shifted his grip to get more comfortable. "Not long now. We're getting closer to the town of Faenza. We'll find shelter soon, I think."

I hope. But hope, like salt, was a precious commodity and equally hard to find.

When they crested the second hill, he spotted a small farm, every bit as run down as Francesco's. Yet the sight warmed Nico all the same. He moved toward it, sending up another prayer for Paolo and the men caught in the mountains, fighting for their lives.

Outside the glow from the house, he set her on her feet, his arms shaking and nearly numb from the exertion. "Let me knock on the door alone. If there's trouble, I want you to run," Nico told her.

To his dismay, she refused to budge from his side, staying with him as he approached the house. The stubborn set of her jaw told him it would be useless for him to argue.

He knocked on the door, the sound hollow. Would he find another miracle of shelter?

The door opened to reveal an old couple, both with white hair.

"What do you want? We have nothing that Mussolini hasn't taken already. I have no animals and no bread," the man snapped as he pushed his wife behind him.

"Shh," the old woman chided as she tapped her husband's arm. "You must not say such things so loudly."

"We do not ask for food," Nico told them. "We need shelter for the night. We've walked a very long way, and we are exhausted." The old man's ire with Mussolini made him breathe a little easier. "Please. My..." He paused and glanced at Sophia, who pulled her coat up to her chin. He noticed the missing buttons. No wonder she shivered so.

"Your wife," the man supplied, his tone softening. "You clearly are not soldiers. Come in. I have a warm fire."

Nico hadn't the heart to argue with the idea of Sophia as his wife, but as he reached for her, he noticed a faint blush staining her cheeks.

"It's Christmas Eve, and here you two are alone with nowhere to go," the woman fussed as she ushered them inside. "No one should be out on such a night. I sense a storm coming, and my bones never lie."

Nico glanced at their host, searching for any danger and finding none within the kind expression. "I am Nico, and this is Sophia."

"Welcome to the Bussepo home. I'm Ricardo, and this is my wife, Angelica. We haven't much, but we'll share what we have with you."

To his surprise, a few hens waddled past him, clucking their dismay.

"We keep the hens in the house so that no one will steal them," Ricardo explained.

The couple led them to a narrow table where two bowls of steaming soup waited. His stomach growled loudly. He hadn't eaten anything in hours. Nor, likely, had Sophia.

The Bussepos treated Nico and Sophia as if they were royalty, giving up their bowls while Angelica grabbed the ladle hanging above the stove. She found two small chipped bowls and poured the last of the soup into them, far smaller portions than those given to Sophia and Nico. Nico protested, but Angelica flapped a hand at him.

Nico's heart swelled when the older couple joined them at the table. He had thought humanity lost, that the darkness had overcome the light, but he had been wrong all along. The light might be harder to find these days, but it was still there, shining steadily.

"You will stay the night here," Ricardo told them. "The weather is getting worse, and there are too many soldiers out there for my liking. You are not with them, are you?"

"No," Sophia answered firmly. "We are not with Hitler or Mussolini."

"I didn't think so, but one can never be too certain. The Germans came through the surrounding villages, pulling as many able-bodied men as they could find to fight the Allies. You're one of the fortunate. Far too many young Italian men have been sent to work for the state in exchange for food."

The rest of the evening passed by the fire as Ricardo shared stories about the way Italy once was.

A simple Christmas, with no tree to adorn the meager space. The cottage consisted of two rooms, an open living space that held the kitchen table and stove and a fireplace, and a small bedroom to the side.

Nico took the painting out of the satchel and brought it to the couple. By now, the frame had taken quite a beating. But he loved it all the more, and he wanted to share it with his hosts.

They took turns admiring the artwork, forgetting the old Italy and the new Italy, and remembering the Savior who came during perhaps one of the darkest seasons of history.

Ricardo sang "Ava Maria," and Sophia sang current Christmas songs she had heard on the radio. The hens fluttered about the room until they settled in the corner, nestling in a worn shirt. The older couple brought them some extra blankets and a pillow for Sophia, then headed into their bedroom.

Silence filled the room, except for the crackle of smoldering logs in the fireplace.

Nico took Sophia's hand. "I wish I had a gift for you." I wish I could save your brother.

She squeezed his hand. "Your friendship is gift enough. I am very grateful for you, Nico."

"I don't deserve such grace," he said. "I've been a coward for far too long. I've never forgotten how you stood up to Matteo all those years ago when we were children. If only I had a touch of your courage."

"You do. It simply looks different than other kinds of courage," she assured him. *"It is because of your past work that you were able to be so helpful to Paolo and our cause. You will keep finding the courage you need in the days ahead of us."*

He continued to hold her hand as they sat by the fire. *"Can you tell me what you did for the resistenza? Why Matteo seemed to single you out?"*

She paused for a long moment, her features soft in the glow of low flames. *"I had an aunt by marriage who became like a mother to me after mine passed. My aunt was Jewish. When General Kesselring ordered the clearing of the Jewish neighborhood, the Portico d'Ottavia, she knew her days were limited. I couldn't let anything happen to her, so I helped her escape. After that, I joined the resistenza, sending coded messages throughout the city. Since I delivered bread to Mussolini's men, I heard many interesting things. My deliveries gave me an excuse to run all over the city. All the while, I thought of my aunt and prayed for her safety. There were so many others like her who needed help, especially after the Germans arrived. How could I stop fighting? Wouldn't you give everything to save the ones you love?"*

Her eyes shone bright in the flickering firelight as she studied him.

"I would," he answered thickly.

Those same beautiful eyes widened, perhaps with understanding.

He glanced away before he made a complete fool of himself. "I wish I had done more when Mussolini came to power. My brother warned me of Italy's fall, but I refused to listen. We said harsh things to each other. I couldn't understand why Alberto abandoned his homeland, why he ran away from me and our family. But he knew what was coming, like you, and he knew he couldn't keep living with integrity if he stayed. Of course, my nonna was adamant to stay in Rome. I felt I had no choice but to do the same. Perhaps if I had tried harder to convince her to leave, she might have. Now, all I wish is to mend what once was broken. To ask Alberto's forgiveness. To somehow find him in America."

"Family bonds are not so easily broken, Nico. He might be thinking of you, praying for you this very moment."

She loosened her fingers from his, and he immediately felt bereft of her comfort. She took the pillow and one of the blankets, then curled up on the floor nearby. He sat by the fire, listening to the pop and hiss of the wood, and found that Sophia's words brought him fresh hope.

Nico rose before dawn. So much had happened so quickly since Sophia's return. He pocketed a little money from his satchel and left Sophia and the couple sleeping. Only a hen fluttered her wings at Nico's movements as he slipped into his boots.

He would replace the food they had eaten. From the conversation the previous night, he knew which direction the village lay. When he approached the town, the gray dawn warmed to tones of pink as his boots crunched on the frosted gravel.

Would he find any food, or would this village prove as bare as the rest? There were no tanks or signs of soldiers, but the stores remained dark and quiet, except one that combined a post office with a general store.

He pushed open the warped door. A middle-aged woman nailed a sign to a wall. Her salt-and-pepper hair was caught in a handkerchief. She was so busy with her task that she didn't notice Nico at first.

The crude writing, however, took his breath away.

Wanted: any members of the resistenza, to be reported to the nearest polizia.

He stiffened as the storekeeper turned around and caught him staring. Somehow, he managed to stutter out a request for supplies and forced himself to wait as she handed him rice. He also found salt, which remained extremely rare.

"Is there trouble nearby?" He pointed to the sign.

"Arrests happen everywhere," the woman said as she took his money and stuck the bills into her dingy apron pocket. "Anyone reporting the resistenza will be paid with extra rations. The polizia and the Germans have set up checkpoints nearly everywhere, so anyone who sides with the rebels won't get very far. If I find one of those traitors, I'll hand him or her over without thinking twice. We could all do with more food in our bellies."

"You're right. I'll keep my eyes peeled, for certain." He forced himself to take the supplies and walk calmly out of the store.

By the time he reached the farm, the morning had dawned bright and clear. The older couple made breakfast out of leftover rations, including several eggs. It looked like a feast to Nico.

"You will stay?" Ricardo asked, eyeing Nico's bag of supplies.

An innocent question. Nico took in the hens and the meager table. "I wanted to replace some of the food we ate last night. We are grateful for your hospitality, but we will leave as soon as we can. How far is it to Bologna?"

Paolo had mentioned that Bologna remained a northern stronghold for the *resistenza*.

The old woman and her husband exchanged a meaningful glance. "Quite far," she said. "And a cold walk. You should be careful. Some young men go north and never return home."

Sophia pulled Nico aside. "I'm not sure we should risk staying any longer than necessary," she whispered. "We'll endanger this couple if we do."

He nodded. "Plus, Paolo said one last message waits. How can either of us abandon him now?"

She glanced over her shoulder at the old man, who reached out to pet one of his hens while his wife puttered about the stove, humming a song.

With one smooth move, she pulled Nico's head down and whispered the message into his ear.

He gasped despite himself.

She released him, blinking back tears. "Now do you understand why Paolo and I have tried to keep our secrets? There are bigger things afoot than our safety. We must warn the Allies as soon as possible. I must do it in person if I can," she whispered.

He kept his volume low as well. "I saw wanted posters. The Germans hunt for the *resistenza*. I can't let you go alone."

She squeezed his hand. "We'll go together to Bologna. There is no one else I would rather have by my side in this. But we must mail your painting to someone you trust to keep it safe. Matteo might know my contacts by now. We need a backup plan in case anything happens to us."

A breath escaped him as he racked his mind for such a person. His neighbor, Mia, likely remained in hiding. The street where he lived must be watched by Mussolini's men. Was there anyone he could trust?

Late that night, after the old couple went to bed, Nico took the frame apart while Sophia wrote the message on a final scrap of paper with his pencil stub. She rolled it tight and tucked it into the slot in the frame. Now that he knew the message, he understood why Sophia dashed across the city with her bakery deliveries, serving the Germans and Italian secret police alike. He knew the extent of her excruciating burden.

With his pencil stub, he gently traced a series of faint lines pointing to the glowing star at the top of the canvas, then added the words, Ecce ad astrum. *Behold the star.*

Would Alberto see the writing and follow the pencil marks up to the star? He couldn't make the message too obvious in case the Germans unwrapped the painting at the post office. Somehow, he had to make everything seem innocent. A simple Christmas gift. He could only hope his brother would figure out his message and warn the proper authorities. He couldn't think of anyone else he could trust, especially now that his band of brothers in the mountains might be no more.

One more Christmas miracle, *he prayed.*

Peace flooded him as he fit the frame together with the newly stretched canvas while Sophia watched him work.

He glanced at her, her dark hair wispy and short. The winsome style was growing on him, much as he'd loved her flowing locks.

Giving in to an impulse, he set down the painting and cupped her cheek. "I don't know what the future will hold, and in case something happens beyond our control, there's something I've wanted to tell you ever since we were childhood friends. I have always—"

He stopped, perhaps out of old habits. He reminded himself to have courage and took a deep breath before continuing. "If I can get you to the Allies, then I'll do everything within my power to see you safe to deliver the last message. Sophia, I have long admired you. I have never met anyone quite as brave as you. Perhaps I'm a fool, but I love you. I think I have always loved you, mia carissima." My dearest.

His confession hung between them, and he withdrew his hand. But before he could say another word, she leaned forward and pressed her lips against his. Surprise rippled through him, and then he pulled her close. The war no longer existed, and all the pain and suffering disappeared in one exquisite moment.

When she drew back at last, her eyes sparkled, and she beamed at him—something he had not witnessed during the past two years. "I love you too, Nico. Since we were children."

Hope and joy crested within him despite the dangerous journey ahead. If God could make a way for His son to escape to Egypt, then tenderly provide for all of humanity to find forgiveness and redemption, then surely Nico could trust that same heavenly plan with his life and Sophia's.

As he fell asleep next to the fireplace, his last waking thought was that Alberto would no longer think ill of his younger brother.

CHAPTER TWENTY-SIX

Debbie climbed into Greg's truck on Thursday morning shortly after the plows cleared the roads. The storm hadn't been as bad as the forecast had warned, but it had still left plenty of snow behind.

As Greg drove from her house, she called Ian and let him know of the exchange she'd had with Jude and her intention to talk with Maurice. Ian promised to meet her and Greg there with Deputy Vaughn.

At the bed and breakfast where Maurice was staying, she and Greg trudged through thick drifts to the large brick house and rapped on the front door.

Maurice greeted them at the door, suitcase in hand. Behind him, several *Days of Yesteryear* staff waited, each with winter coats and plenty of luggage.

"I'd like to chat before you leave," she told him without preamble.

"Debbie Albright." Maurice gazed past her. "You brought the police?"

She glanced over her shoulder to see Ian exit his cruiser, wearing his full uniform and a pair of aviator shades. He appeared downright intimidating this morning despite his bout with the nasty cold. Deputy Brendan Vaughn climbed out of the passenger seat, every bit as formidable as his boss.

"Yes. I need to ask you some questions about the derailment and the missing painting. Did you arrange them?"

"Not much subtlety from you, I see."

"I missed my coffee this morning, so you'll have to excuse my bluntness," Debbie replied, refusing to be cowed. "Did you arrange for the tracks to be diverted? My understanding is that someone tampered with the switch, which derailed the train. And since you plan to air the bad footage, I have to believe your desire for ratings and profits overrules your common decency, which means I can't put anything past you."

Maurice frowned. "Have you been speaking with Jude?"

Ian approached the wooden steps. "Mr. Devons, before you leave, we need to chat."

"All right, though I fear Debbie has beaten you to the interrogation." Maurice set his expensive designer suitcase on the snow-covered steps. "I did not arrange for the train to be derailed. I've never spoken to Leo regarding derailments and train rides. I have not taken the painting. Feel free to search my luggage and that of my staff. We've been snowed in, so I would have had no opportunity to dispose of the painting to a buyer. Please, check our cars and the bed and breakfast. Investigate my staff as thoroughly as you would like. We will fully comply."

Debbie glanced at Greg, wondering if it was a trick of some kind.

But Ian didn't even need to order the bags open. Maurice flipped open his suitcase, his face white, while his staff followed suit with their luggage. "I don't need this kind of publicity. My career is already ruined."

"What do you mean?" Debbie frowned.

"I've gotten word that someone will replace me as the face of *Days of Yesteryear*. Oh, and they plan on renaming the show. Something British, I guess. Less Americana charm and more of a focus on rare finds overseas."

The hair on the back of her neck rose at Maurice's admission. "Overseas antiques, you say?" She scanned the *Days of Yesteryear* crew, searching for two faces in particular—and finding neither. "Where are Jude and Victor?"

Maurice shrugged. "Off to get one last order of mochas from your café, I guess. Then we'll hit the road if your chief of police will let us go."

Ian straightened from one of the open bags before him. "I can't assess everything out here. I need you all to come to the police station with me. We'll need additional statements from everyone."

"Gladly," Maurice said somberly. "I have nothing to hide. Yes, I did ask my crew to get footage of the train during the derailment. I've never lived through anything quite so frightening and wanted it chronicled. As a TV and social media personality, I live for ratings. I'm ashamed to say that Debbie was right in her assessment of my ambition outweighing my good sense. I am truly sorry." Maurice lowered his voice as he climbed down the slick steps in his cowboy boots. "I didn't mean to ruin anyone's Christmas. I promised to air a good show, and I will keep my word. I wish you the best, Debbie, both to you and your man."

As Maurice passed her, she glanced at the steps, noting Maurice's classic cowboy imprint in the fresh snow. It didn't match Ian's photo of the footprints out by the switch. As the crew filed one by one, she discreetly checked the prints left by their sneakers and boots. None of them left the heavy tread marks Ian had discovered. Nor did the open bags of the crew reveal a painting.

Ian had already moved to the crew's cars to peer inside, and Brendan entered the bed and breakfast.

She mulled over the conversation. One man had control over the cameras, and he had been very helpful sharing his footage. Leo also remained a possibility.

"Still think Maurice did it?" Greg asked Debbie as the TV show's vehicles roared to life all around them. With Ian's police cruiser nearby, she didn't think anyone would bolt. If anything, Maurice appeared determined to clear his name.

"No. I don't think Maurice took the painting or caused the train accident. I think the derailment appears to have been planned by someone very clever with a flair for the dramatic. Greg, I need to get to the café. Can you drive me there?"

When Debbie pushed open the door to the Whistle Stop Café, her heart nearly stopped. Leo and Ricky sat at a table in the corner. Both men had a cup of coffee and a cinnamon roll. In front of Ricky lay several faded documents.

"Am I seeing things early this morning, or are you two actually having coffee together?" Debbie asked as she unwound her scarf.

Ricky appeared almost sheepish. "I went through my grandfather's file cabinet again, just to make certain, and I found a copy of the will. He did leave the painting to me in the official will, but later he wrote a letter to Leo, stating the Nativity was to go to him. Sadly,

Grandfather never got his will updated, so I can see why Leo thought the painting was his. He assumed it would be in the will, so he didn't bring the letter with him at the time. But he has it now. The dates on both documents make what happened clear as day."

Leo shifted in his seat. "Grandfather told me he would put the painting in my name. Ricky made an innocent mistake, and we took it too far, arguing over who got what during the inheritance when we should have been focused on coming together as a grieving family. Ricky called me last night to ask me to meet him and discuss everything."

"I'm sorry we let things get so strained," Ricky told him. "And now the painting has been stolen. It's bad enough that you haven't had it all these years when you were supposed to, and now I can't even make things right by giving it to you."

Leo clapped his cousin on the shoulder. "I'm sorry too. It's just stuff in the end. I don't know why it took so long to get it through my thick skull, but after the derailment, I realized I have what matters most—my health and my family. I was always saddened by Grandfather's relationship with Uncle Nico. They never spoke again after Grandfather left Italy. No one should be separated forever because of an argument."

"I'm glad you two are finding some closure," Debbie said as she headed to the kitchen.

"So they're friends again?" Greg asked under his breath as he followed her.

"I think so," she whispered back. "I'm glad they resolved their issues."

But seeing Leo with Ricky also made it less likely that Leo had stolen the painting. Didn't it? She frowned as she entered the kitchen.

Janet pulled a tray of scones from the oven. "Hi, Debbie. And Greg. What a nice surprise. How did the conversation with Maurice go?"

"He left willingly with Ian. I guess Maurice might lose his job to someone with an interest in European antiques," Debbie said.

"I'm just here to say hi," Greg added. "And check on what your specials are this morning. Is it too soon for scones?"

"I've got one saved for you. Make yourself at home at a table, and I'll bring you coffee too," Janet answered him.

As Debbie hung up her coat and pulled on her apron, she heard the bell jingling above the front door. All the while her mind whirled, replaying what Maurice had shared. She sent a quick text to Ian regarding her concern about the cameramen, but she didn't expect to receive a reply. He must be busy talking to Maurice and the crew.

As she poured Greg's coffee, she recognized a familiar form with a tweed jacket and corduroy slacks approaching the glass display. Jude studied the menu board and the cake doughnuts.

"Hi, Jude," she said, attempting to keep her voice friendly. "How did your chat go with Maurice about quitting the show?"

"Hey." He smiled at her, his eyes crinkling at the corners. "I lost my courage. Maybe I'll tell him when we get back to the studio. I have to share a rental car with him and a return flight home in first class. I'm sure you understand my hesitancy."

"Of course. Can I get together some mochas for you and your fellow cameraman?"

"Just for me, but I'll also take doughnuts for the road. Make it a box, Debbie. I'm famished."

"Where is Victor?" Debbie asked as she loaded a white pastry box with a baker's dozen. She slid the box into a plastic bag.

Jude plunked money onto the counter. "Victor wanted one last shot. It's been quite a trip, and I'd like to have some pretty film of the snow falling near the station."

She handed him the bag and the steaming mocha, along with the change. "Still planning to head to Miami?"

"I can't wait to wear shorts and flip-flops again," he said. "Keep the change, please. You've been so great about everything. And have a merry Christmas. I won't forget this place, and I'm sure the Whistle Stop Café will charm all of America when the show comes out."

"That's great news," she said, mentally scrambling for ideas on how she could stall him. "Let me get the door for you." Her gaze fell to the black mat where a clump of snow melted in a clear footprint. It was the same tread that Ian had snapped a photo of the day of the train derailment.

Her heart sank.

Greg had joined Leo and Ricky in conversation. She tried to catch his eye without alarming Jude, but to no avail.

She would have to follow Jude out into the cold. "I'm worried about how Maurice will respond to you quitting. He's at the police station now with the rest of the crew. Our police chief might want to chat with you further."

"I've given them my statement," Jude said breezily as he fished in his pocket with one hand while holding the mocha and bag in the other. "I've got nothing to add." He scooped out a set of keys and hit the button on the fob. A van chirped, signaling that it was unlocked.

She was out of time and options. She prayed someone would see them through the window.

"I don't know about that," she replied, hoping she sounded braver than she felt. "I think you could provide some extra-colorful details."

"Oh?" he asked brightly.

"Definitely, since you had plenty of opportunity to case the joint before you derailed the train and stole the painting. I'm not sure which one motivated the other. It's a chicken-and-egg problem. Did you plan to steal the painting all along and derailed the train to further that cause? Or did you take the painting to distract from the train derailment? And why would you choose to derail a train if distraction was the goal? To make your boss look bad? To get wild ratings for the show? Regardless, Jude, people could have been seriously hurt—or worse. You realize what you did will be considered a federal crime, don't you?" Debbie folded her arms across her chest to keep the chill away.

He stopped, his back to her. Then he turned slowly. The mask fell, and he bared his white teeth into a snarl. "Don't you dare accuse me of derailing a train. Maurice is the villain here, not me. He's so desperate to land a second season on TV that he'll do anything for ratings. He's stolen antiques before, and he'll do it again. No doubt he and Leo worked something out to derail that train. Maybe they hired someone to steal that painting."

She shook her head. Jude had constantly tried to fill her thoughts with suspects. Leo. Maurice. Brad and Tim. All in attempts to divert attention from himself and Victor, while trying to appear helpful by sharing footage.

"Our police chief took photos of footprints by the switch. With a distinctive tread, probably from some heavy boots. Boots like the ones you're wearing right now. The tread matches the police photos." She gestured behind them at the footprints he'd left. "Plus, you had help. Victor, I'm guessing. You flipped the switch, and he took the painting. Perhaps you edited the video footage, changing the time stamp. How lovely of Kim to give you access to the entire station. That must have made it so much easier to carry out your plans."

"You can't prove anything," he growled.

By now, she had followed him far enough that Greg and the other men couldn't easily see her from the café windows. The wind whipped her apron, and she shivered, partly from the winter weather but mostly from the deadly glare Jude angled at her.

"Open your trunk. Let's see what you've got."

Rolling his eyes, he approached the driver's side of the van. "This is ridiculous, Debbie. Go back inside before you get sick from the cold."

She darted to peer through the van's window and there, behind the driver's side, she caught a glimpse of an ornate frame. Even though she expected it, a thrill shot through her, and she gasped out loud. Victor sat in the passenger seat, his eyes wide with alarm.

A hand clamped around her upper arm in an iron grip and dragged her away from the van. The ice on the pavement made her slide all too easily.

"I warned you, Debbie!" Jude hissed.

She kicked him in the shin as hard as she could. He grunted and dropped the mocha to the ground. His hold on her arm loosened enough that she was able to yank free.

He lunged at her, his eyes bulging and a vein popping at his forehead. "I'll get you for that."

"No you won't. You won't ever touch her again," Greg bellowed. He charged across the parking lot with Ricky, Leo, and Janet right behind him. Greg planted himself between Jude and Debbie, hands on his hips as he faced the cameraman.

Ricky and Leo flanked him, cutting off Jude's chance of escape.

Jude raised his hands, his rage replaced by surrender.

"I'm calling Ian," Janet panted as she pulled out her phone.

"Good. Because I found our painting and our saboteur," Debbie said. She glared at Jude around Greg. "It just goes to show that you shouldn't take advantage of good people. It never works out in the long run."

Jude hung his head.

CHAPTER TWENTY-SEVEN

"Package for you," the postmaster told Alberto Carosi, *sliding a battered package with stained brown paper across the counter.*

Alberto reached for it, his heart stuttering when he read the Italian address. A sliver of unease wrapped around his heart.

"Sorry about the delay. I think it got held up at customs. You know how things are these days," the postmaster added with a lopsided grin.

Alberto understood. Anything from Italy meant a government inspection, along with plenty of suspicion. He felt the paper, noting the hard ridges beneath his fingertips. The stamp showed the package had been mailed December 27th of the year before last. At once, he thought of his brother, Nico.

When Alberto arrived home, his nephew Rafe and Rafe's new girlfriend, Eileen, waited in the living room. Once a month, he held a dinner party at his house, inviting neighbors and friends for pasta and tiramisu.

He stood in the living room with the package pinned awkwardly beneath his arm.

"What are you doing, Alberto? Put that package down and join us," Eileen told him with a twinkle in her eye. As stationmaster at the train depot, she was used to giving commands.

He sighed, fully aware that he could hide nothing from his family and friends. He ushered her and Rafe into the kitchen. "I just got this. It's from Italy."

Rafe inhaled sharply.

When he peeled the paper away, he found the image of a beautiful woman staring back at him. Mary cradled a baby Jesus while the star of Bethlehem shone bright above her.

A hush fell over the room as they all gazed at the artwork. The picture appeared worn. Tired. The frame had gouges and dirt streaked across the canvas. Even the gold gilding had begun to wear off, yet *he would recognize Nico's talent anywhere. Mary beamed at him, her triumphant smile reaching Alberto's heart.*

"Nico," he whispered as he touched the painting.

"Who is Nico?" Eileen asked with a frown. "It's a gorgeous piece."

When Alberto couldn't respond, Rafe explained, "Nico is Alberto's brother, still living in Italy. Alberto hasn't heard from him in a long time."

The uneasy glance Rafe cast Alberto said even more. The two Italian men understood better than most what Alberto's brother would have faced in fascist Italy over the last several years. No note accompanied the artwork. Was Nico safe? Why would he send the painting after years of silence?

The faint lettering traced on the surface of the painting puzzled him. Behold the star.

He studied it, absorbing the colors and lines. So much talent wasted on the wrong cause for so many years. Did this Nativity mean that Nico had changed? And if so, why no note to accompany it?

Alberto remembered the ugly words he and Nico had exchanged at their last meeting. How the two of them had fought, flinging accusations at each other, chipping away at family bonds.

If only Alberto could go back. If only he could tell Nico that he loved him and didn't care about anything but reforging their bond.

Alberto closed his eyes and prayed for his younger brother so far away, with an ocean between them and so much more. He prayed that his brother, the prodigal son, would somehow find his way home again.

CHAPTER TWENTY-EIGHT

Thursday morning passed by in a blur as they watched Ian and Deputy Vaughn place Jude in the back of the police cruiser. Ian shut the door while Jude glowered from behind the glass window.

Hours later, that same cruiser parked at the café, and Ian climbed out, then reached back into the vehicle and removed the painting. He entered the café, pulling off his sunglasses to reveal dark circles beneath his eyes, but his easy smile brought a sigh of relief from Debbie.

Leo and Ricky waited at the table along with Janet.

"I'm returning something that belongs to you," Ian said to the Carosis as he carefully placed the painting on the table.

Ricky beamed at him. "I thought we'd never see it again. What happened?"

"Victor and Jude confessed to everything," Ian explained. "When Maurice gushed over the painting, they decided to take it. Victor snuck into the café to change the camera angles. He tried to sneak in again after the play rehearsal."

"Why did they want to steal it?" Debbie asked.

"Since Maurice thought it was valuable, they thought it would be easy money. Jude also saw the perfect opportunity to frame his boss or perhaps Leo. Plenty of people, including Jude, witnessed Leo and Ricky's argument."

"That's true," Leo said with no small amount of chagrin in his voice.

"Early the day of the train ride, Jude headed out to switch the tracks. Later, Victor loosened the ropes for the pen to create a distraction at the café. Between the train derailing and animals escaping into the parking lot, Jude pushed a table against the kitchen door and grabbed the painting. It's small enough that he could tuck it into his coat. He ducked into Kim's office and made sure the security footage didn't show him taking the painting, then stowed the art in his vehicle and got back into the chaos of the day. Victor covered for him while he was gone. He and Victor played with their footage afterward and gave me a falsified version. Jude also dropped plenty of hints about his terrible boss. He wanted everyone against Maurice so he could steal the show for himself."

"Jude tried to steal a painting and a show?" Ricky frowned. "Now that's a terrible employee."

Ian nodded. "This painting has been through quite an adventure."

Ricky gently touched the frame. "Thank you, Ian. Thank you, Debbie. I can't tell you what it means to me to have this restored to the family."

Ian took a seat and cleared his throat, his voice gravelly. "I can't say much about the derailment investigation. The feds have taken over that, and I've done all I can."

"I'm guessing Jude saw that as an opportunity to take the painting and frame his boss. If Maurice went down, Jude hoped to steal his show as well as the painting," Debbie added. "Everyone could see how enamored Maurice was with the Nativity."

"There is something special about it. I've always wondered about the markings leading to the Bethlehem star, though," Leo said.

"Me too," Ricky agreed. "Debbie and I wondered if perhaps Nico didn't get a chance to finish it as he wanted to."

Leo frowned as he studied it.

"The Latin phrase on the manger translates to 'Behold the star,'" Debbie explained. "What do you think Nico meant by that?"

"I always thought a message lay within the painting," Leo said. "Those arrows pointing to the star seem to be in pencil rather than paint. I could only think of two reasons for that—either the painting was unfinished, or it held a secret message."

"Maybe there really is a message in the painting," Debbie said. "I've been reading about the Second World War in Italy and how the Italians were divided in their loyalties. The Partisans sent messages to one another in code."

Leo traced the frame with a finger. "It's true. A vast underground network of resistance fighters refused to follow Mussolini. They found places in the caves and the mountains, in the cities and villages, hiding from the Germans. When Mussolini faced capture by his people, Hitler invaded and took over Italy. Meanwhile, the British and the Americans landed at Sicily and pushed north. The fighting proved intense until, at last, Mussolini and Hitler were both defeated." Leo paused, as if lost in thought. "Nico stayed in Rome because his grandmother refused to leave. Alberto and Nico fought over it and never spoke again. Yet in 1945 Alberto received this painting, sent from the area around Bologna in December 1943. Why would Nico leave Rome?"

He nudged the picture toward Ricky, and the frame popped loose.

"It definitely needs some restoration," Janet observed.

The canvas slipped free, revealing a gap in the wood.

"Look above the star," Debbie said, pointing.

Ricky tugged off the top of the frame, freeing the canvas. Something yellowed with age lay within a carved hollow inside the wood.

Ricky used his finger to slide out the object. "It's paper, rolled tight."

"Do you think you could open it?" Janet asked. "We would love to know what it is."

He unfurled it, scanning the faint scrawl of handwriting. "It's in Italian."

Leo held out his hand. "May I see it?" His brows lowered as he studied it.

Everyone else watched him impatiently.

Finally, Leo raised his head, his eyes glowing. "This is amazing. It says, 'Alberto, I have been outside of Brisighella with the resistance. I'm heading to the nearest British line to ask for their help. You were right to leave Italy when you did. I'm sorry that I didn't listen to your warnings sooner. I never imagined that I would end up feeding the Fascist propaganda machine by making posters for them, but they threatened Nonna, so I had no choice. I've done what I can to make amends, helping Jewish families escape and sending messages for the resistance. Remember our neighbor, Sophia Guidice? I've fallen in love with the bravest of women, who helped the Fatebenefratelli Hospital hide Jewish families. Forgive me. One of my greatest regrets is our last meeting, when we fought. Know that I will always love you. I hope one day you will be proud of me again. Your brother, Nico.'"

Ricky gasped and covered his mouth. "All that time, Nico longed to make amends, to reconcile."

"It appears your great-uncle was a hero," Debbie said.

"I've heard about the Fatebenefratelli Hospital," Leo said. "The hospital administrators invented an illness called Syndrome K that they claimed was highly contagious and deadly, but it was actually code for a Jewish person that they were helping. The Nazis steered well clear of it, and the doctors were able to hide perfectly healthy Jewish Italians in the wards."

Debbie pulled out her phone and did a quick search for the hospital. "It says here that the hospital became a haven during the Nazi raid of the largest Jewish community on October 16, 1943. You said Nico mailed the painting in December, correct?"

"Of 1943," Leo confirmed.

"If only Alberto had found the message. Did the hospital survive the war?" Janet asked.

Debbie scrolled through the article. "Germans deported over a thousand Jews from Rome to Auschwitz, but three thousand men, women, and children remained in hiding until the Allies stormed Rome on June 4, 1944, and freed them. The hospital played an integral role, saving several hundred lives."

"I think this painting was used to transport hidden messages," Leo added. He separated the rest of the frame from the canvas, holding up the wood pieces. "Lots of nail holes where someone disassembled and reassembled the frame over and over."

"Did he make it to the British army?" Ricky asked. "And who is Sophia?"

"I couldn't find his name anywhere online with previous searches," Debbie added.

"Can we find a Sophia Carosi online?" Janet asked.

Everyone got out their phones and tapped away.

"Still nothing," Debbie said, shaking her head.

"What if they changed their names like Eileen's husband? Rafe Palmer was shortened from Rafaello. He tweaked it to better fit in with Dennison and his Marine division," Ricky pointed out.

"What if we search for artists from World War II-era Britain?" Debbie suggested.

Like a key into a lock, the search finally yielded results. Debbie found an article on a Nicholas Carras, a wartime artist who specialized in propaganda posters. She held her phone so all could see. "What do you think? Could he be your great-uncle, Ricky?"

Ricky took her phone. His eyes welled with tears. "Yes, that's him. Older, but that is Nico Carosi. He looks so much like…"

"Like you," Leo told his cousin with a hint of awe.

"It says he moved with his wife to London and lived there until he passed in 1948," Ricky read. "It's so sad that Nico died thinking that Alberto got his message and didn't respond."

Silence fell over the group as they considered Ricky's comment.

At last, Ian pushed away from the table. "It's still an amazing story to share with your family. It's a good reminder that relationships are important, and we need to give grace and mercy with family. If you don't mind, I need to fill out some additional paperwork before I head home to enjoy my own family." He bent and kissed Janet's forehead. "See you at home, sweetheart."

Debbie felt a ping. Not jealousy. She'd never be jealous of her best friend's happiness, but that simple statement awakened a quiet longing in her. She thought of Greg at home with Jaxon and Julian. Family was truly a gift to be cherished. Nor could she deny any longer that she wanted that with Greg.

A sigh escaped her, but any sense of wistfulness fled when Ricky and Leo stood. "I want you to have the painting, Leo," Ricky told his cousin. "It's only right. I've enjoyed it for many years when it shouldn't have been mine, and now it's your turn."

"We should make a print of it. And our families could take turns housing the painting," Leo replied. They embraced, and when Ricky handed the painting to Leo, something shifted in the room. Something beautiful that brought tears to Debbie's eyes as well.

"Merry Christmas, Leo," Ricky said.

CHAPTER TWENTY-NINE

A soft snow fell on Christmas Eve. "O Holy Night" played over the speakers while Debbie sat on the couch with Greg, Julian, and Jaxon following a wonderful supper of ham, mashed potatoes, various salads, and plenty of raspberry thumbprint cookies. Hammer, Greg's faithful border collie, was curled contentedly at his feet. Her parents had joined them for the festivities, along with Paulette. The gifts made a cheerful pile under the Christmas tree. She couldn't wait for the boys to open them the next day. In addition, they had enjoyed the local Christmas Eve service, lighting candles and singing carols before heading home.

Now, after plates of homemade caramels and a special dish of tiramisu from Ricky, Debbie savored this blissful moment of enjoying family. Greg's tree sparkled in the corner of the living room, where the popcorn strings and country ornaments scattered with precious mementos brought a special touch.

"Aren't we going to watch the Christmas special from *Days of Yesteryear*?" Debbie's mom asked.

"I can't wait to see my daughter and her café on TV. I'm so proud of you, Debbie," Dad said from one of Greg's comfy chairs.

Greg switched on the TV and found the episode with his remote, then slung his arm over Debbie's shoulders, drawing her close.

To everyone's delight, *Days of Yesteryear*, hosted by a rather subdued Maurice Devons, showcased all the best of Dennison, from the snow-covered streets to the stained glass windows of the depot. Everything appeared so charming, especially the children giggling as they petted the donkey and the bleating sheep. There was a close-up of Nico Carosi's painting. The video cut to a puff of steam from the train engine as it chugged out of Dennison, heading into the winter landscape.

Maurice appeared at the end of the special, dressed in black, but with a green bolero tie. "Folks, by now I'm sure many of you have heard about the derailment that occurred in Dennison, Ohio. Although no one was hurt, we lost something very precious that day."

Debbie agreed with that. She'd lost much of her faith in her fellow man. In the days that had followed Jude's arrest, Debbie had learned that he would face an array of federal charges, but it didn't undo that he had risked so many lives for his own selfish reasons.

"I'm asking for your help to restore a national icon, rich with history," Maurice continued. "I'm donating one hundred thousand dollars to fix or replace the damaged trains, and I hope you'll consider donating as well. Dennison's legacy belongs to all of us, and it's our responsibility to preserve its history so we can entrust it to future generations. During World War II, Dennison acted as a hub for our brave soldiers heading out to fight for our freedom. We cannot let such a heritage be forgotten or ruined. Any donation you can provide will go directly to fixing the trains."

"I didn't know he was doing that," Paulette said. "How lovely."

Maurice's trademark smile returned. "And I hope you will join me in the new year as we rediscover the United States on a victory tour, examining lesser-known World War II sites…"

Greg turned down the volume as the show ended. "Maurice got to keep his show, after all."

"Yes, and Kim told me he's already delivered the money he promised in that clip to the museum to help with the trains. I'm grateful he gave us good coverage," Debbie said.

"Janet must be so pleased to see the matching aprons and shirts on TV," Paulette said, grinning. "We should open an online store and sell them."

Debbie laughed. The conversation continued around them until she heard Greg clear his throat beside her.

"Will you take a walk with me?" he asked in a low tone. "I have a gift for you, and I want to give it in private, but I don't want to wait until tomorrow."

Thoroughly intrigued, she got up and followed him to gather their outer layers and duck out into the night.

Outside, a white moon broke free of the clouds, illuminating Greg's street in a silvery glow that made the snow sparkle. The wind whispered through the trees and tossed powdery flakes on their way down. She drew the cold air deep into her lungs, admiring the colored Christmas lights casting a glow of red, green, and blue in alternating patterns against fresh snowbanks. It was a magical night, full of promise and joy.

Greg paused, turned her toward him, and pressed his forehead against hers. "Debbie, that day when we got off the train, you said you didn't want to imagine life without me."

"I did," she whispered, almost forgetting to breathe.

"I can't imagine my life without you either. Ever since you returned to Dennison, you've changed everything for the better. I've thought of nothing but you since the train accident. Life is too short not to say what's been pressing on my heart."

She waited, holding her breath.

He kissed her, a heart-melting kiss that made her pulse take flight.

When he finally broke the kiss, he whispered what she had longed to hear. "I love you. I didn't think it was possible after I lost my wife, but you make everything feel possible."

"I love you too. I never dreamed I would find someone like you," Debbie answered. "I'm grateful for all the amazing gifts that have come into my life here, but you and your boys are the greatest gift of all."

He brushed his lips against hers again, and a feeling of belonging settled inside her, permanent and secure.

He pulled a long, thin velvet box from his pocket. "Maybe I should save this for tomorrow morning, but it made me think of you, and I can't wait another moment to give it to you."

Inside the box, a line of white fire flashed and gleamed in the moonlight. It was a diamond bracelet, so exquisite and bright that she could only stare at it in wonder.

"Oh, Greg," she whispered. "It's stunning."

"It reminded me of a star," he murmured as he reached for her again. "For the woman who is the star that leads me home."

She lost track of the minutes after that, at least until her nose and fingers chilled and neither she nor Greg could stay outside any longer. As they approached the house, the picture window in the living room depicted a beautiful scene of the people Debbie loved—her parents, Paulette, and the boys laughing as they played board games beside the Christmas tree.

Greg opened the door for her, his eyes twinkling.

She gazed upward to the ceiling, where a mistletoe spun lazily above them. Peggy Lee crooned "Winter Weather" in the background. He kissed her again, leaving her breathless.

"Okay, lovebirds, that's enough. You're letting in all the cold air." Debbie's dad chuckled.

Unable to stop smiling, Debbie soaked in the precious scene before her, trying to memorize every detail to cherish later. Everything she had ever needed or wanted was in that living room. God had provided above and beyond anything she could have ever expected.

Debbie slipped her hand into Greg's strong grip. He loved her. With a heart as steadfast and patient as his, she was truly home.

Dear Reader,

I hope you enjoyed the taste of Italy threaded throughout *Winter Weather*. As always, I gravitate to stories of strong women in history. Did women actually fight in the resistance movement during World War II? Yes, countless women were instrumental in France and Italy, and several rose to a level of leadership previously unheard of.

Many Italians hated what happened to their Jewish neighbors. They hid Jewish families in monasteries and convents, in the basements of churches and homes, and even in a hospital in Rome. One brave doctor invented the idea of Syndrome K to keep the Nazis from entering a wing of the hospital where Jewish families hid. Within the city of Rome, over a thousand Jews were deported to the German concentration camps. Few returned. The rest remained hidden in Rome thanks to a few brave Italians who passed secret messages back and forth, letting Jewish families know where to hide.

For example, Carla Capponi, nicknamed "the Little English Girl," led the resistance with great courage, becoming vice commander of the Gruppi di Azione Patriottica. She was one of fifteen women to be awarded the prestigious Golden Medal of Military Valor. Her introduction to the resistance occurred within a sculptor's studio, of all places. Art, after all, has the power to move the heart and soul.

I find the story of average Italians and Americans choosing to do what is right in the face of darkness to be so encouraging. No matter our current circumstances, the hope and beauty of Christmas lives on.

Blessings,
Jenelle Hovde

ABOUT the AUTHOR

*J*enelle Hovde writes gentle stories of redemption and hope. She lives in Florida near the beach where she homeschools three girls. When she isn't writing, she manages two spoiled cats who insist on catching lizards. Her other cozy mystery fiction includes *We'll Meet Again* and *A String of Pearls* with Guideposts' Whistle Stop Café Mysteries series.

TRUTH BEHIND the FICTION

*A*rtists have always played an important role in society, even if one conjures the image of a starving creator. Hitler and Mussolini strove to create an art movement including architecture, art, music, and film to convince the masses of the superiority of their brand of government.

Mussolini led first, later inspiring Hitler to release such propaganda in Germany. They idolized certain forms of beauty while destroying art they deemed unworthy. Today, tourists can tour Mussolini's buildings and film studio, which is still in use.

Other artists fought against the rise of oppression. In the 1930s, with the rise of dictators, Picasso created works of anti-nationalism in Spain. A more famous American version of propaganda included Rosie the Riveter with her cheerful, "We can do it!" sentiment to encourage women to step outside of strict gender roles.

Governments understood the power of art. Whoever controlled the media controlled the message. In the United States, the Office of War Information formed in 1942 with the purpose of creating a cohesive message for the public, comprised of posters, pamphlets, newsreels, radio shows, and movies, each medium designed to stimulate a patriotic response to the war effort.

Although art was used during the Great Wars for both good and terrible purposes, a few brave artists designed something unusual.

Camouflage became a necessity during World War II. Solomon J. Solomon, a member of the Royal Academy in Great Britain, developed a realistic camouflage netting as a method of covering trenches. In addition, he created the ingenious and deceptive "observation tree," a hollow replica tree trunk placed in enemy territory, from which a scout could survey the trenches without detection.

Another artist, Normal Wilkerson, created a dazzle camouflage to protect the ships in the ocean by painting them with zebra stripes to hide the ship's movements. Other methods included painting the ships the color of the sky to blend better. Fake shadows confused the enemy reconnaissance planes, suggesting weapons that might not be on the ship while concealing artillery. A decoy of six hundred fake tanks fooled the enemy into assuming an attack could happen at any moment.

A new type of soldier found themselves recruited to fight in World War II. Cartoonists, stage designers, movie writers and producers, and magicians were prized for their skills in visual trickery.

Each one served as best they knew how, with the pen sometimes proving to be mightier than the sword.

FROM the HOME-FRONT KITCHEN

Italian Christmas Ice Cream Cake

Trade the standard cookies and tarts for an icy treat consisting of the simple ingredients listed below. Layer pints of softened ice cream with coffee-soaked ladyfingers, and finally top with sifted cocoa powder. This Italian ice cream cake offers an *easy* alternative to baking!

Ingredients:

2 pints tiramisu or vanilla flavor ice cream

1 pint cannoli or coffee flavor ice cream

2 packages ladyfinger cookies

1 cup strong coffee or espresso

1 tablespoon cocoa powder

Directions:

1. Soften ice cream for 10 to 15 minutes.
2. Spread first pint of tiramisu or vanilla ice cream in bottom of a 9×9-inch pan.
3. Pour coffee or espresso into shallow bowl. Soak half the ladyfingers in the coffee, then arrange over the ice cream.
4. Spread the pint of cannoli or coffee-flavored ice cream over soaked ladyfingers.

5. Add another layer of soaked ladyfinger cookies over second layer of ice cream.

6. Spread remaining pint of ice cream over soaked ladyfingers. Cover dish with plastic wrap and freeze for 4 hours. Sprinkle the top with cocoa powder before serving.

WAIT TILL THE SUN SHINES

BY MARGARET WELCH

t looks like every kid's idea of a treasure chest." Janet Shaw, her eyes wide, took in the size of the antique box with its arched top. "Do you know how Ian would describe it?" she asked, speaking of her police chief husband.

"I'm all ears," Kim Smith said.

"It's big enough to hide a body."

Kim laughed. "If it held a body, trust me, I would have invited Ian instead of you and Debbie." Kim, director of the Dennison Depot Museum, had asked her good friends Janet and Debbie, co-owners of the café situated in the depot, to come feast their eyes on the contents. Janet had arrived in the museum workroom first. "Where's Debbie?" Kim asked. "Should we wait for her?"

Janet was itching to peek inside but said, "She'll be here any minute. After church, she and her parents joined the residents of Good Shepherd for Sunday lunch." Until he'd retired, Debbie Albright's father had been the director of Good Shepherd Retirement

Center in Dennison. "Did someone really drop this beauty at the museum and say, 'Here. Have a treasure chest?'" Janet asked.

"Pretty much," Kim said. "Not to burst your bubble, though, it's technically a steamer trunk."

"But you said it has treasure in it," Debbie said as she bounced through the door. "I'm all agog."

"I can now give you the official details." Kim took a paper from her pocket. "Twenty-nine inches high in the center of the lid. Thirty-four long and twenty-two deep. The hardware is brass. The handles on each side are leather. The black slats on the top and sides are... I don't know what kind of wood. Maple or oak, maybe."

Janet walked around the trunk. "It conjures all kinds of stories about romantic foreign travel, doesn't it? I wish it had destination stickers all over it. Any idea how old it is? Who donated it?"

"I can answer one of those questions with confidence," Kim said. "A woman named Dawn Anderson. She isn't local, but she's been in town off and on over the last few months clearing out a deceased in-law's house. She was here when that television crew came to town to film for the *Days of Yesteryear* show."

"Gotcha," Janet said. "She caught the same bug everyone else did and hoped the trunk was more special than it is."

Debbie patted the trunk. "I think you're special even if the TV people turned up their noses."

"Mrs. Anderson said she wasn't surprised the TV people didn't exclaim over the contents," Kim said. "She thought the museum might be interested in them, though. I thanked her for being community minded. Then I told her the museum would accept the donation but only with the stipulation that we can dispose of any part of it that we can't use for the museum's collections. Again, she didn't seem disappointed."

"She doesn't want any of it back?" Janet asked.

"She says she's up to her eyeballs in stuff and 'so over' the idea of any more stuff," Kim said. "As for how old the trunk is, after a quick bit of research my guess is 1930s. Possibly '40s, though, considering what's inside."

"Which is?" Debbie asked. "Come on, Kim, how long are you going to torture us?"

"Be tortured no longer." Kim, with her flair for dramatics, lifted the trunk's lid. "Voilà. We have an amazing assemblage of 1940s women's clothing."

"Ooh!" The exclamation came from Janet and Debbie at the same time.

"May we?" Janet mimed taking the clothes out and holding them up.

"Be my guest," Kim said. "Take them out and lay them on the worktable as you go. There are a few other things mixed in with the clothes, mostly toward the bottom, that I haven't looked at yet."

"How could you resist? I mean, look at this." Debbie held up a white cotton dress with a dirndl skirt. Three rows of red rickrack edged the square neckline and the cuffs of the short, puffy sleeves, and also outlined the shape of a faux apron on the skirt.

"There's all kinds of adorable things in there," Kim said, "and I wanted to share the fun of discovery."

Janet held up a robin's-egg blue shirtwaist dress covered in large white polka dots.

"Can we keep them?" Debbie asked. "I mean the museum, not us."

"Although…" Janet batted her eyes, making Kim laugh.

"Sadly, nothing in the trunk fits the museum's collection policy. Even sadder, as much as I love 1940s styles, none of the clothes fit *me*. But," Kim said, giving them a conspiratorial look.

"But what?" Debbie asked. She laid the white dirndl on the work-table and picked up a wool blazer and houndstooth wool skirt.

"But I can see that you're as smitten as I am. I hoped you would be, because I have an idea."

"Take the day off and play dress-up?" Janet took a pair of elbow-length white calfskin gloves from the trunk and held the soft leather to her cheek. "Please?"

"Better than that," Kim said. "Let's have a—"

"Fashion show!" Janet and Debbie said at the same time then looked at each other and laughed.

"Great minds," Kim said. "Exactly what I was thinking. We can charge a fee to attend and split the proceeds between the museum and the café."

"What a great way to beat the January doldrums," Debbie said.

"Perfect," Janet said. "But can we pull it together fast enough to have it this month?"

"Again, great minds," Kim said. "We wouldn't *have* to do it this month, but it'd be a wonderful draw. We know January weather in Ohio goes from iffy to icy in a blink. Not the best month to attract out-of-town visitors. But a fashion show would bring in locals too."

"Especially if we ask locals to model," Janet said.

"So why don't you look through the rest of the trunk," Kim said, "and make sure our rose-colored glasses aren't skewing our judgment. I'll be back in a few. I need to make a call."

Janet and Debbie took turns removing items from the trunk, bringing out dresses, skirts, blouses, trousers, a handknitted sweater, a few hats, two pairs of shoes, and several more pairs of gloves.

"Because a woman just wasn't dressed to go out if she didn't wear gloves," Janet said, adopting a prim pose.

"They weren't wearing those gloves when they stitched these." Debbie lifted a stack of what appeared to be unassembled quilt blocks out of the trunk. "How cool is this? Each square has a different name embroidered in the center of it."

Kim appeared in the doorway.

"Did you see these?" Debbie held up the squares. "Look how pretty they are."

"These were at the bottom?" Kim took the pieces. "I'm sure the fabric is cotton flour sacking. But how often do you see pristine quilt blocks from that period?"

Janet scooted closer to see. "Do you recognize any of the names?"

"A few," Kim said. "They've passed, though."

"This reminds me of the time capsule we opened last year," Janet said. "Names and possessions from out of the past, each with a story."

"They're called signature quilts," Kim said, "and they have stories to tell. They were often made by a group of friends or church members as a going-away or wedding present." She fanned through more squares. "There ought to be a Bible verse or some kind of congratulations or farewell message on one of these. A date too." A frown line appeared between her eyebrows. She looked quickly through the two or three dozen blocks again then shook her head.

"That's disappointing," Janet said. "But we can give the blocks an approximate date from the names. Maybe the fabric too?"

"True." Kim brightened. "And because there are local names, that means these were probably made right here and the quilt was meant for someone in Dennison. It might be a fun project to locate any of the quilters still with us. Or relatives of those who've passed."

"Fun for a volunteer?" Debbie asked.

"For me," Kim said with a grin. "I love quilts even if I don't quilt, and I love this kind of social history."

"Try to find out why it wasn't finished," Janet said.

"It makes you wonder, doesn't it?" Kim asked. "A lot of work went into these blocks."

"It did," Janet said, "and why they never became a quilt might be an interesting part of their story." She watched Debbie take a tailored skirt and blouse from the trunk, and then she took her turn. "Here's the last and possibly least, considering how worn the material is. Oh." She looked up. "It isn't clothes. Something's wrapped inside the cloth. Have you seen this, Kim?"

"I didn't even make it as far as the quilt blocks. I assume that's more flour sacking, though."

"This is as much fun as guessing a Christmas present." Janet lifted the wrapped bundle out of the trunk and ran her fingers all around the shape. "It feels like a small box." She gently shook the object. "There's something inside." She carefully unfolded the fabric. "Oh my. I think it's—" She gently shook it out and held up a faded, mended, obviously much-loved and often-used apron made of yellow, red, gray, and white plaid fabric.

"It's darling!" Debbie said.

Janet let Debbie take the apron from her. While Debbie and Kim exclaimed over its somehow unfaded brightly colored binding, she examined the small box she'd unwrapped. A hen and a rooster, painted on the top, looked back at her. On the front face, written in black lettering, was a word dear to her heart—*Recipes*. She swung the hinged lid open to see dozens of recipe cards and immediately started flipping through them.

"Have you ever seen an apron pattern like this?" Kim asked. "Aren't most of yours sort of rectangular?" The apron she held up was all curves. The bottom edge, rather than cut straight across, was rounded like a smile. The top of the bib was another curve, made large enough so that instead of a strap or tie for behind the neck, the seamstress had simply cut a hole big enough for the cook's head to pop through.

"I never have," Debbie said. "Seems very retro. Not retro back then, though, I guess. The yellow and red are perfect for the café, don't you think? It's like it was made for our decor. Wouldn't it be fun to make a couple of aprons like it? Does anyone make reproduction flour sack fabric?"

"Someone must," Kim said. "What's the box, Janet?"

"Something that might be even better than the apron." Janet held the box to her heart. "It's a file box. With handwritten recipes from dozens of women including..." She stopped then continued with a hitch in her voice. "Including Faye Canby, my grandma. It's her recipe for dream bars. She made them when I was little. I haven't had one or thought of them in years."

"With a name like that, are they as dreamy as they sound?" Kim asked.

"As far as I remember."

"Do you recognize any other names?" Kim asked.

"Come see." Janet patted the floor next to her. No way was she handing the recipe box to someone else before she'd seen every card. They flipped through them together, laughing at some of the odd-sounding recipes, pointing out those they'd enjoyed or avoided at community potlucks. They only recognized a few of the contributors.

"There's no name that tells you who the box belonged to?" Kim asked.

Janet examined the box, inside and out. "Nothing." She quickly fanned back through the recipes. "Some of the cards have women's names on them, but not all. At a guess, the cards without names were written by the owner. Because who would bother to write their name on their own recipe?"

Janet looked up to see Debbie smoothing a small stack of papers. "What have you got, Debbie?"

"The sweetest notes," Debbie said. "They were tucked into one of the trunk's side pockets. They're written by two different people— on each note, one person wrote the first few words and a second wrote the rest."

"Person A and Person B," Janet said.

"Spoken like the wife of a police chief," Kim said.

Debbie sorted through the notes. "Sometimes Person A starts the note and sometimes Person B does. Listen to this one. Person A writes, 'Have I told you lately,' and Person B writes, 'that I love you.'"

"That's charming," Janet said. "Read another."

"Person A writes, 'You're only'," and Person B writes, 'as pretty as you treat people.'"

"I like that one nearly as much," Kim said. "But it almost sounds like the beginning of a joke. How many people does it take to write a—how many words in that note?"

Debbie laughed and counted. "Eight. How many people does it take to write an eight-word note?"

"The paper's yellowed," Kim said. "Maybe the notes are left from a 1940s or '50s party game. One person starts and another person finishes a well-known saying."

"That could be fun," Janet said. "I'd play."

"Oh, but here's the best one so far." Debbie held up a note then read it. "Person A writes, 'You are,' and another person, not B, based on the handwriting—"

"Person C?" Janet supplied.

Debbie nodded and handed the note to Janet. "It seems to be a child just learning to print. Person A writes, 'You are,' and Person C prints, 'my sunshine.' You were right when you said we'd find all kinds of adorable stuff in the trunk, Kim. This note is *every* kind of adorable. Thanks for sharing this with us."

"But now we've reached the end, haven't we?" Kim sighed. "No more surprises, except that the bottom of the trunk is covered with awfully pretty flower-sprigged paper."

"This doesn't look right," Janet said. She reached inside and pressed a finger on the bottom where it met the side of the trunk. It gave a little at her touch.

"What do you mean?" Debbie asked.

Janet rapped her knuckles lightly in several places on the bottom inside the trunk. "It doesn't sound right, either. Listen." Kim and Debbie leaned in as she rapped again. "I think it's a false bottom."

"There's a stub of ribbon in the back left-hand corner," Kim said. "See if you can get hold of it and pull."

Janet pinched the ribbon tightly and tugged. She felt resistance then movement, and with another tug, the bottom came away. Beneath lay a white box that fit perfectly into the hidden space.

"I did not see that coming," Kim said. "You found it, Janet. You open it."

"I will not say no to that." Janet took a deep breath then lifted the lid of the box. Whatever lay inside had been carefully wrapped in tissue paper. She just as carefully folded the tissue back, revealing a white dress. "Do you think it's a wedding dress?" she asked. "It looks almost too pretty to take out of the box or touch."

"But should we anyway?" Debbie asked.

"Are you kidding? Of course," Kim said. She fished a pair of cotton museum gloves from a pocket. "With these."

"You do the honors." Janet moved aside and let Kim take over.

The dress Kim lifted from its nest of tissue paper took Janet's breath away. Tea length, with a pleated skirt, it had a fitted waist and bodice with lace and beads across the shoulders.

"Early '40s, I think," Kim said. "Stand up, Debbie." When she did, Kim held the dress up to her. "Like it was made for you. You should model this in the fashion show. Can't you see it, Janet?"

Busy staring at another slip of yellowed paper, Janet didn't answer.

"Earth to Janet," Kim said. "What have you found now?"

"Another note. It fell from the dress when you held it up. A dress, by the way, which will look gorgeous on you in the show, Debbie. This note is from one person only. It says, 'But still my fancy wanders free through that which might have been. Thomas Love Peacock.'"

"Wow," Debbie said. "Not the kind of note you expect to find with a wedding dress."

Kim laid the gown back in the box and smoothed the bodice. "Ladies, I think there might be yet another note." She lifted the dress out again and looked at the inside of the bodice. "A pocket. Whoever heard of a pocket in the bodice of a wedding dress?"

"It's over the heart," Janet said. "Is there a note in it?"

Kim pulled a folded paper from the fabric and handed it to Janet.

The cold heart of winter stole from me,
but life goes on as you shall see,
and someday, dear, in love you'll be,
and wear this dress instead of me.

"There's a story here," Kim said, "and I, for one, want to know what it is."

"It's more than a story." Janet looked at Debbie. "See if you can finish this sentence. I love a—"

Debbie grinned. "Mystery. Let's call the donor."

Janet pulled out her phone and waggled it at Kim.

"Her number's in the office," Kim said. "Let's go get it."

After tapping in the phone number, Janet held her breath and waited for Dawn Anderson to answer. She gave her friends a thumbs-up when a woman's voice said hello in her ear. "Mrs. Anderson? My name is Janet Shaw. I'm calling from Kim Smith's office in the Dennison Depot Museum. She and a friend of ours, Debbie Albright, are here too. We've been looking at the trunk you donated and wonder if you know that it has a false bottom?"

"You're joking." Dawn laughed.

"No." Janet couldn't help grinning.

"Is there anything in it?"

"Another dress," Janet said. "A special dress."

"Unless it's special because it has pockets, and the pockets are stuffed with twenty-dollar bills, I'm not interested in more clothes. Make that hundred-dollar bills. A twenty doesn't go far these days."

"Sorry." Janet laughed. "There is a pocket, a *hidden* pocket, but no money. Next time you're in town, why don't you come see it?"

"I'm in Dennison now and will be for a couple more days. But is it really worth my time?"

"I tell you what," Janet said, looking at Debbie and Kim. "Debbie and I run the Whistle Stop Café here at the depot. Come for lunch tomorrow, our treat, and see what you think. How does twelve thirty sound?" Debbie and Kim nodded enthusiastically.

"Might as well," Dawn said. "They say free food tastes better, don't they? I'll let you know if it's true."

"Wonderful. See you tomorrow."

When Janet disconnected, Debbie asked, "What's that look on your face?"

"Confusion," Janet said. "I can't tell if Dawn is a kidder or unusually candid." She repeated Dawn's remarks about hundred-dollar bills and free food.

"You should have told her it's a wedding dress," Debbie said. "And about the secret message *in* the pocket. Why were you so cagey?"

"I think I got rattled," Janet said. "It's silly of me, but there was something oddly familiar in her voice. And it made me want to be cautious."

A NOTE FROM the EDITORS

We hope you enjoyed another exciting volume in the Whistle Stop Café Mysteries series, published by Guideposts. For over seventy-five years, Guideposts, a nonprofit organization, has been driven by a vision of a world filled with hope. We aspire to be the voice of a trusted friend, a friend who makes you feel more hopeful and connected.

By making a purchase from Guideposts, you join our community in touching millions of lives, inspiring them to believe that all things are possible through faith, hope, and prayer. Your continued support allows us to provide uplifting resources to those in need. Whether through our communities, websites, apps, or publications, we inspire our audiences, bring them together, and comfort, uplift, entertain, and guide them. Visit us at guideposts.org to learn more.

We would love to hear from you. Write us at Guideposts, P.O. Box 5815, Harlan, Iowa 51593 or call us at (800) 932-2145. Did you love *Winter Weather*? Leave a review for this product on guideposts.org/shop. Your feedback helps others in our community find relevant products.

Find inspiration, find faith, find Guideposts.

Shop our best sellers and favorites at
guideposts.org/shop

Or scan the QR code to go directly to our Shop

While you are waiting for the next fascinating story in the Whistle Stop Café Mysteries, check out some other Guideposts mystery series!

SECRETS FROM GRANDMA'S ATTIC

Life is recorded not only in decades or years, but in events and memories that form the fabric of our being. Follow Tracy Doyle, Amy Allen, and Robin Davisson, the granddaughters of the recently deceased centenarian, Pearl Allen, as they explore the treasures found in the attic of Grandma Pearl's Victorian home, nestled near the banks of the Mississippi in Canton, Missouri. Not only do Pearl's descendants uncover a long-buried mystery at every attic exploration, they also discover their grandmother's legacy of deep, abiding faith, which has shaped and guided their family through the years. These uncovered Secrets from Grandma's Attic reveal stories of faith, redemption, and second chances that capture your heart long after you turn the last page.

History Lost and Found
The Art of Deception
Testament to a Patriot
Buttoned Up

Pearl of Great Price
Hidden Riches
Movers and Shakers
The Eye of the Cat
Refined by Fire
The Prince and the Popper
Something Shady
Duel Threat
A Royal Tea
The Heart of a Hero
Fractured Beauty
A Shadowy Past
In Its Time
Nothing Gold Can Stay
The Cameo Clue
Veiled Intentions
Turn Back the Dial
A Marathon of Kindness
A Thief in the Night
Coming Home

SAVANNAH SECRETS

Welcome to Savannah, Georgia, a picture-perfect Southern city known for its manicured parks, moss-covered oaks, and antebellum architecture. Walk down one of the cobblestone streets, and you'll come upon Magnolia Investigations. It is here where two friends have joined forces to unravel some of Savannah's deepest secrets. Tag along as clues are exposed, red herrings discarded, and thrilling surprises revealed. Find inspiration in the special bond between Meredith Bellefontaine and Julia Foley. Cheer the friends on as they listen to their hearts and rely on their faith to solve each new case that comes their way.

The Hidden Gate
A Fallen Petal
Double Trouble
Whispering Bells
Where Time Stood Still
The Weight of Years
Willful Transgressions
Season's Meetings
Southern Fried Secrets
The Greatest of These
Patterns of Deception

The Waving Girl
Beneath a Dragon Moon
Garden Variety Crimes
Meant for Good
A Bone to Pick
Honeybees & Legacies
True Grits
Sapphire Secret
Jingle Bell Heist
Buried Secrets
A Puzzle of Pearls
Facing the Facts
Resurrecting Trouble
Forever and a Day

Find more inspiring stories in these best-loved Guideposts fiction series!

Mysteries of Lancaster County

Follow the Classen sisters as they unravel clues and uncover hidden secrets in Mysteries of Lancaster County. As you get to know these women and their friends, you'll see how God brings each of them together for a fresh start in life.

Secrets of Wayfarers Inn

Retired schoolteachers find themselves owners of an old warehouse-turned-inn that is filled with hidden passages, buried secrets, and stunning surprises that will set them on a course to puzzling mysteries from the Underground Railroad.

Tearoom Mysteries Series

Mix one stately Victorian home, a charming lakeside town in Maine, and two adventurous cousins with a passion for tea and hospitality. Add a large scoop of intriguing mystery, and sprinkle generously with faith, family, and friends, and you have the recipe for *Tearoom Mysteries*.

Ordinary Women of the Bible

Richly imagined stories—based on facts from the Bible—have all the plot twists and suspense of a great mystery, while bringing you fascinating insights on what it was like to be a woman living in the ancient world.

To learn more about these books, visit Guideposts.org/Shop